A Handbook for the Spiritual Traveler

In a world where people are earnestly trying to understand why the world is the way it is, and are beginning to look at their own religious upbringing and the effect it has had on them – the Good, the Bad and the Ugly – Riaz shows great heart and unyielding passion in not only discovering, but sharing the fruits of his own intense search for spiritual and religious Truth. For those who are looking to claim their own Truth and Faith – Riaz's story is both personal and engaging – why not step inside and see for yourself? There may just be some answers to help you find your way.

Valerie Simonson
Bestselling Author of *Orange Socks – How a Yuppie Goes Yogi.*

A Handbook for the Spiritual Traveler

Riaz Manji

Stepping
Stone
Publishing

www.steppingstonepublishing.com

National Library of Canada Cataloguing in Publication Data

Manji, Riaz, 1958-
A handbook for the spiritual traveler

Includes bibliographical references.

ISBN 0-9730535-0-X

1. Spiritual life—New Age movement. 2. Self-actualiza-
tion (Psychology) 3. Spiritual biography. 4. Manji, Riaz,
1958- I. Title.
BL73.M36A3 2002   299'.93   C2002-910251-0

Editing: Leslie Johnson
Page Layout and Design: Sage Creek Books
Cover Design: Jon Paine
Author Photograph: David Watt
This book was printed and bound in Canada by Friesens
Corporation for Stepping Stone Publishing.

Stepping Stone Publishing
P.O. Box 84122
Market Mall RPO
Calgary, Alberta
Canada
T3A 5C4
www.steppingstonepublishing.com
info@steppingstonepublishing.com

Names Declaration

This is a true story. However, some names of the people in this book have been modified to safeguard their privacy. I have used the generic name "church" to denote a place of worship. My intention is not to disrespect nor show preference to any particular denomination or persons.

Dedication

This book is dedicated to my mom, Khatie.
She was a humble woman who died as she lived — with grace, courage, strength and an immense faith in God.

Acknowledgements

First I would like to thank God for helping me throughout my life and especially for His assistance in the last ten years. In writing this book, I required a lot of help. I found that He was always there to assist me and for that I am extremely grateful. Big thanks to my mom, Khatie, for always being there to provide love and help throughout my life. She had tremendous inner beauty and she radiated humility, courage and willpower. She was a wonderful mentor and I looked up to her. To Leslie Johnson, an editor who performed above and beyond the call of duty. If I took all the languages in this world that had the word "thank you," my appreciation would still not be expressed properly. Your guidance and inspiration touched my heart and your friendship and commitment will never be forgotten. My sister Rozy took care of me and fed me while I was writing this book. You have been a tremendously positive force in my life and I look forward to enjoying your friendship for many years to come. Some of my family members appear in my book. To them I say, thank you for your contributions and assistance throughout my life. My other family members and friends have indirectly or directly helped me throughout my life and in writing this book. To them I want to say that good friends are hard to find and I respect and admire each and every one of you. Thank you to Valerie Simonson for her ongoing help and feedback. Finally, I want to thank all the authors who have written the many books that have helped me in my search for the meaning of life. Books have provided me with immense knowledge and have increased my spiritual growth immeasurably. Although many authors have been influential, the works of Edgar Cayce and Shirley MacLaine have been extremely important and have affected me deeply. A big "thank you" to both of them.

Contents

Introduction

When you sell a man a book you don't sell him just twelve ounces of paper and ink and glue — you sell him a whole new life.
— Christopher Morley

This book is the story of my journey of Self-discovery. Until I was thirty-three years of age, I was heavily involved in organized religion. I thought that I knew myself – and my place in the universe – well. I also believed that I was a spiritual person because I attended my church regularly. At the time, I was convinced that being religious and spiritual was the same thing. But I was wrong. I almost attempted suicide and this crisis caused me to look in the mirror and ask myself those tough "meaning of life" questions: What is life all about? What is the purpose of our being here?

The great humanitarian, Mohandas Gandhi once said, "We must not, like the frog in the well who imagines that the universe ends with the wall surrounding his well, think that our religion alone represents the whole Truth and all others are false." In 1991, after my desire to commit suicide, I began to read books about Self-development and spirituality. I felt I had to increase my spiritual knowledge. I also started to establish a personal connection with God through meditation and prayer. The personal and spiritual growth that I gained through doing these two things has made me a much happier individual. I know that I would have had a more difficult time coping with challenges such as family illnesses if I had not learned about the existence of our Spirit and the true eternity of life. Since we all belong to the same spiritual family, I believe that many people share the questions that I had about our purpose in life.

And so many of the answers that I found may also benefit many people as well. I hope that the knowledge that I have gained in facing the challenges in my life will also help you deal with the adversities that you face in your own life.

When I started searching for answers to my questions, I discovered that I needed to revisit my past. So in the first section of my book I take you back to my roots in Africa. Then we will go to the heart of England where my family moved after leaving Africa and then to my present home in Canada. In the second section of my book, I will tell you about the spiritual knowledge that I gained through my journey of Self-discovery. If you have spent most of your life following the practices of an organized religion, as I have, perhaps this knowledge will help you explore other avenues of thought.

Throughout my life, I have found that there are many people who have not found all their spiritual answers in their respective religious or spiritual practices. As a result, they have explored other alternatives and new spiritual groups have been created. This new spirituality has often been described as "New Age" thought. But this spiritual knowledge is not really "new." Although this esoteric and metaphysical information has become prominent in the last thirty years, this knowledge has been available to us for centuries. New Age thought has been defined as the relearning of ancient wisdom. It seems that many of us, living in this technological age, have forgotten the age-old teachings that explain the basics of our life here on Earth. These essential teachings tell us about the importance of connecting with our higher Spiritual Power. It is this connection that enables our souls to grow spiritually. I believe that we all need to *embrace* our spiritual path – whatever that path may be. Life itself, and our spiritual path in particular, is an adventure, and every step that we take along that journey takes us closer to our spiritual fulfillment, and therefore closer to God.

One person who played a major role in my spiritual journey is my mom, Khatie, and so I would like to dedicate this book to her. She was a wonderful person and I looked up to her. My mom was always very supportive of me, and I shall never forget her loyalty and her dedication to me. Khatie had cancer for thirteen years. She had a strong faith in God, which helped her get through her long and painful illness and the many challenges in her life. She was a very strong person but she was also humble at the same time. About ten months before Khatie passed away, she had a near death experience. At that time my mom was told to go back to Earth because it was not the right time for her to come to the spiritual realms. She remained on Earth for several months longer, and I looked after her. During that time, I felt strongly motivated to write this book. The knowledge that I gained on my spiritual journey helped me cope with my mom's illness and deal with her passing. Now that I know that the Spirit is Eternal and that life is a journey, I know that her passing is just another step in her evolution – towards God and her own enlightenment. Sometimes I wonder if part of the reason that she remained on Earth for a little while longer was to give me the opportunity to write this book. That possibility alone has made writing this book a very personal and important task for me. I believe that life is full of connections. Things do happen for a reason. Perhaps there is a reason why you are reading this book right now. I know that life is also full of challenges, change, and growth. I am sure there is much more to explore and learn and I look forward to my journey. I hope that, in some small way, this book also helps you in your own journey through life.

Section 1

My Story

For what is it to die but to stand naked in the wind and to melt into the sun? And what is it to cease breathing, but to free the breath from its restless tides, that it may rise and expand and seek God unencumbered?

— Kahlil Gibran, *The Prophet*

I went through my episode of desiring to commit suicide in the summer of 1991. It was late in the evening and the air felt dry and cool. The summer sun was dissipating and apparently, so was my life. Although a few friends and family knew about some aspects of this episode, I was not comfortable talking about it for the fear of ridicule. I felt people would look down on me and see it as a weakness. Therefore, I never gave them all the details and feelings of this life-altering event. Writing this book has allowed me to talk about it openly, to anyone. What is my motive? Simple, to make sure no one else commits suicide! If I can save one life with the words on the following pages, I would be one happy man! Hopefully, I can help many people with this information.

At one time or another, I am sure all of us have thought about ending it all. We may feel "What is the point to all this?" It's better to die than to live with this pain! Well, I know that feeling quite well. Before 1991, my lifestyle was structured with lots of religion and sports especially tennis

3

as a major part of my life. Sure I had fun but I think I had lost contact with my soul and God. I did not know myself that well. Ever since I was young, I always had questions about spirituality. Why are we here? What is our purpose in life? What is death? Where do dead people go? Why do people get diseases? But, I never got my answers. Maybe I did not look in the right places. I never read books at that time but asked other people these kinds of questions. I asked spiritual elders, and my friends and family but they did not have the answers. Well, at least none that would satisfy me! Before I explain more about my desire to commit suicide, I will give you a little bit of my history. As you may see, my past has many symptoms that had contributed to my suicide attempt.

I was born in Tanzania, East Africa in the spring of 1958. My family was one of the richest and reputable families in my small town. At that time I had no idea that the wealth would be short lived. When I was about seven years old, this classmate who was a few years older than me bullied me a lot. I was the African Elephant and he was the rider with the cane. He was probably imitating the actions of a popular comic strip character and his elephant that was popular at that time. Regardless, I never enjoyed this abuse. I hated it. He used to ride me and whip me pretty hard. This happened several times. I remember coming home crying to my mom many times. I was hoping that she would get my brother to beat him up or at least allow me to take some kind of revenge on him. "What should I do, mom?" My mom, Khatie, did not believe in violence and she did not say much. She just consoled me the best she knew. Today, I still feel anger towards that guy. If I ever see him again, I will give him a whipping. Well, maybe not! I guess I am more spiritual now, so I should try to forgive him! As a result of this abuse, I felt I lost some self-esteem. How can people be so cruel? Why pick on me?

I don't remember much hugging or affection in our family. Even now, I don't think we hug that much. There is always support but little or no physical affection. Even now, I know we care and love each other a lot, but we don't really say it out loud that often. Maybe words are not required. Khatie and my father, Hassan had an arranged marriage. Khatie was always supportive, kind and generous. She came from a poor family and appreciated the value of money or lack of it. She married into a rich family. Once she had told me that before I was born, she wanted to run away and become a nurse. She loved taking care of people. In my hometown she was known as the reliable one. She would help anyone rich or poor. She was also very charitable. But, she was not that happy in her marriage. She was smarter than Hassan in school and had better grades. Women were considered second-class citizens at that time and had their "place in life." They were primarily responsible for bringing up children and taking care of the household. I was never close to Hassan. He was busy in his business and seemed aloof, unapproachable and uncaring. He supplied all the material needs but did not play a major part in my upbringing. He was closer to my sister, Rozy.

Rozy was active in my education. She felt that it was the key to my future. She had missed out on a good education and felt that I should get the best education possible. She hired tutors so that I could get extra help in my studies. I hated studying! I wanted to play sports. Little did I know at that time that education was critical in terms of my future mental discipline. Education meant knowledge. This pursuit of knowledge would be important to me later on in life. My brother, Ali was very active into sports and I followed in his footsteps. I was the youngest one and considered the spoilt one. Strange, but I never felt like a spoilt kid. I was happy in a lot of ways, but I also felt neglected. Was I asking for too much? I was born late and the difference between my next sibling and me, Ali, was about fourteen years. Even though I had friends, I felt very alone, as I had no siblings I could really associate, relate to or play with.

When I was young, I lacked self-identity. Little did I know at that time that it would affect me later on in life, well into my early thirties. Just like any kid, I loved movies. The fact that my family owned a theatre didn't hurt. I spent a lot of time at the movies. I was entertained. Like any kid, I imitated some of the dancers and actors in the movies. I wanted to be the hero that got the claim to fame and saved the world. Once, when I was about eight years old, I saw Rozy shaving her legs. I thought, well I am now a grown up and I should shave mine too! That's what grown ups do, right? I saw some actors in the movies and they had no hair. But, I barely had any hair. I think I can see a few? I wanted to surprise everyone. At dinner, I proudly announced that I had done this. I was expecting applause, hugs and approval from my family. I was ready to take the bows. I felt I would now be welcome into the world of grown-ups. You guessed it, no such luck! I don't think I have seen jaws drop that fast, not even on hungry alligators! There was laughter and ridicule in the room. What did I do wrong? Where are my hugs? I left the dinner table and went to my room. I felt really bad and was very upset for months. I felt embarrassed about that event. Even today looking back on it, I am still embarrassed about it and have never talked about it with anyone. This was not a sex or gender issue. I never thought of myself as a female. Sexually, I am attracted to women and not men. Always have been. This was more about finding my place in the world. Where do I really belong? Who am I? What is right and wrong? Am I doing the right thing in my young life? Once again, I felt alone and that no one understood me.

Once we had some visitors from England. Ali was studying in England and had brought his Danish girlfriend and a couple of friends to Africa for a visit. They were chain smokers and smoked cigarettes constantly. I liked what I saw. I had to try one! It looked like they were having fun. I took the left over cigarette butts; some had lipstick on it but I didn't care. I found one of the Danish girls quite attractive so maybe I would smoke her cigarette. I started smoking secretly in my parent's room. The cigarettes were awful! What did these people like about that? Looking back on that event, I was once again experimenting and trying to find my identity. I guess I wanted to be a grown up. Once when I went to church, one girl came up to me and said, "I like you, you are handsome." I was so happy to hear that. I had no idea I was good looking. That's the first complement I remember getting. I thought to myself, "did my family give me compliments." I don't remember them. I must have gone home and looked in my mirror that evening and wondered what she liked about my features. It didn't matter. I must be good looking. That was a major revelation! I found out something about myself! It felt good.

When I was in Africa, I think I had a creative spark in me. Also, I had a need for adventure and freedom. I did not like to be constricted or tied down. I remember going on long trips with my parents. On those trips, I was bored sitting in the car. I used to look at clouds and try to see shapes in them. I saw elephants, rhinos, giraffes, tractors, cars, people with beards and hats, children and the like. I felt my creative juices working and I noticed my mind was getting massaged. I felt good inside. It felt peaceful. I liked the feeling a lot. Looking back on it now, I think of this time as a form of meditation. It was such a soothing and calming feeling. I could feel it in my soul. I felt connected to nature. Our town was inland. But I loved to visit my eldest sister, Hanna, who lived in the big city. This city was on the Indian Ocean. One look at the ocean and I was hooked. As I looked yonder, all I could see in the distance was water, nothing but water everywhere. I wondered how far the water went. I wanted to explore and go to new lands. What was out there? I wanted to find out. I associated water with exploration and freedom. And freedom to me meant happiness. I was excited! I should have enjoyed that time more because soon my life was going to change in a dramatic way.

In 1971, due to economic and regional problems in Africa, My parents and I moved to Birmingham, England. I was thirteen at that time. One day, while walking to school, I had to walk across a barren field and three boys approached me. The one I remember the most was a scruffy, longhaired, tall boy who looked like "scarface." He wasn't the prettiest to look at but he was definitely the most violent. All the boys hurled "racial abuses" at me and beat me up. Although I tried to cover my face, they must have broken my nose because I was bleeding and had a bump on my nose. To this day, that bump is a reminder of the tough times I went through in England. Once Ali and his girlfriend came to visit us from London. She brought me a souvenir from Scotland. I thought that was nice. But, I cried to her because I was so unhappy. Furthermore, I did not get any attention from Ali as I barely saw him. I felt I had nowhere to turn. I told her not to mention this incident to Ali. I did not want to worry him. To this day, I don't think he knows of this event.

Once Ali came to Birmingham and asked me where I wanted to go. I wanted to see the James Bond double feature. He said he would take me. I was really, really excited. At last I can share something with my blood brother! I never knew him nor shared much with him. I believe the fourteen-year age gap was a factor. This was my chance to get to know him. We went inside the theatre but after a few minutes, he left me. He said he would pick me up after the movies ended. I guess my brother did not want to share a movie with me. I was hurt. It was no fun watching the movie alone. He had paid for the movie, which was nice, but why did he leave me. I felt alone again. Next, I started to write poetry. I was only thirteen or fourteen but felt confident and creative. I was very proud of my writing and felt it had rhythm, substance and depth. I thought it was a good first try. I showed it to my best friend. He thought it was awful! I was really disappointed and felt uncreative and worthless. When was I going to get some positive reinforcement? Can I do anything right?

We owned a small grocery store in the worst neighborhood in Birmingham. We never had a television in my hometown in Africa. Television was something new and exciting to me. I escaped from my unhappy teenage life in England by watching lots of television. The television room was connected to the store by a door. I would laugh so hard at the English comedies that I would disturb the store customers. My father would yell at me to keep my laughter down. But, I felt happy for a change. That black and white screen gave me hope that there was a better world out there away from my dreary, harsh and futile existence. In that television world there seemed to be happiness, laughter, kindness and compassion and understanding. Relationships blossomed, families and their children were happy. Sure, there was sadness and death but people helped each other out. There was generosity and effort to help the meek and the sick. How come I wasn't happy? Maybe television life was not real?

Once while carousing in downtown, I saw a color television in the window of a store. That was first time I had seen a color television in my life! I was fascinated and excited. I stared at that color television for a long time. The storeowner must have been concerned. Whenever I went to town, I stared at that television set from the store window. I wished we could afford a color television, but we were too poor. I loved the beautiful colors I saw on that television set. I needed more color in my life; that's for sure! I wondered what life in color was like. It seemed happier that the black and white version. Once I ran away from home, my piggy bank in hand. I had enough and I was going to leave for good! I felt that no one understood me! I just want to be happy! I had a few English pounds in the piggy bank. I walked around my poor neighborhood for a couple of hours. Where should I go? I thought of running away to London, the big city. I could find a job there. But I was just a teenager. Who would hire me? I came back home looking dejected, solemn and glum.

Sometimes I wonder where I would be now if I had really run away.

I went through puberty and a major culture shock and did not understand the physical and psychological changes occurring in me. Adjusting to a strange land and a lack of self-identity and self-esteem compounded the problem. I used to walk from school to home with my head bowed to the pavement. I was depressed and confused and lacked direction. Once I locked myself in my parent's room and prayed and prayed for help. I also prayed to a spiritual leader. I kissed his picture and asked for assistance. As time went on, I kissed his picture so much I wore it out! Where was I to turn for help? I felt lost and confused.

Where should I go with my questions and problems? Hassan would not be much help as he barely talked to me. Communication between us was pathetic. It was pretty much non-existent. Conversations were out of convenience and necessity. But I could see his situation. He had gone through a major cultural shock as well. Back in Africa, he was the wealthiest man in that town. At one time he was the mayor of that town. Because he hadn't sent any money out of Africa, he came to England with very little cash. That is the how we ended up in that poor neighborhood in Birmingham. Hassan was depressed and wanted to go back to Africa. The economic and political situation was not good in our country so he could not go back. The strong one was Khatie. I was shy and unsure about how to approach her with my questions on puberty and the like. I figured I would do my best. I asked her about my physical and psychological changes. I also told her I could not sleep. She said, "Go to church, you will find your answers there!" I figured, ok, that's where the answers lay. Parents have all the answers, right?

So, from then on, I went to my church every day. Before this, I had already been going to church but not every day. Our church is open every day and we are encouraged to attend the evening service for prayers and the morning for meditation. I was also a "volunteer," which meant that I helped with extra duties such as cleaning the church and helping with church activities. I was the first one into church and the last one out. I also liked helping people and being a volunteer, allowed me to make people smile and make a difference in their lives. I felt a sense of belonging and comfort. I found some peace. The people were from my culture, background and color. At least I would not be exposed to racism at church! Maybe I could get an understanding of why people could be so cruel to each other. Are we not the same inside, in our souls? If you include the day I was born, I went to church for more than 30 years of my life! After a while, I did not think about it too much. Like clockwork and ritualistically, I went to church. It helped in some sense because it gave me an introduction to spirituality, meditation and established a connection to God. But there was still something major missing. I was not completely satisfied inside. I ignored that "gut" feeling and carried on with my routine but yet in many ways a happy life. I was too extreme and lacked balance in my life. But I did not know this at that time.

After more than four years in England I moved to Canada at the age of seventeen. I worked hard, got my degree from university and worked full time for many years. I was involved in a few minor relationships but none that were long lasting or deep. I enjoyed people a great deal. I was friendly and people seemed to like me. As a result, I had many friends and was socially active. But, my life consisted primarily of work, tennis, and religion. In 1990, when I was around thirty-two years of age I got into a very intense and serious relationship with a twenty-two year old girl called Marisa. This relationship was like none that I ever had before. In 1991, after a year and a half, the relationship moved to a higher level. There were talk and preparations for marriage. Marisa and I had good times but we also had a few problems. But they did not seem that major. Maybe they were? But, there was something inside of me that was not happy. Something did not feel right! I was not sure what that was. All I knew is that I was unhappy, but wasn't sure why.

I started getting many speeding tickets. I lacked concentration and focus. I was unproductive at work. I started focusing heavily on my personal relationship. Little did I know at that time that I was focusing on external factors to please me internally. This fulfilled me and gave me a high, but only temporarily. It was like a drug, it gave me a quick fix. Once I was away from my relationship and back into reality I became depressed again. With my confused state, I was making Marisa unhappy as well. She suggested alternatives such as more "space" between us. Another option was temporary separation. I listened but did not implement any of her proposals effectively. I was in no state of mind to do that!

Some of my friends thought Marisa wasn't right for me. Maybe her friends thought the same of me? One thing was certain; I knew I had to get out of this relationship! There was no doubt about that! But, I asked myself, how? There were expectations not only from Marisa but from both families as well. The families thought I was very religious and they were pleased about that. I couldn't make them unhappy, could I? There were people relying on me to get married. Plus, I was now thirty-three. It was time for me to marry, wasn't it? In fact I was already behind in terms of the "normal" marrying age, at least according to government statistics. Most of my friends were married. Some of them already had a couple of children. But I was confused, lacked maturity and did not know my soul or myself as well as I thought I did. I got depressed and felt alone. I could not sleep and felt fatigued. I had nowhere to turn. Marisa and I went to church together in order to find an answer. I sat in church but had a hard time concentrating. I did not seem to feel any better. I felt overwhelmed, lost and without direction. I had suicidal thoughts. I told my family and some close friends about my situation. They helped the best they could. I still felt helpless and worthless. I told Rozy and she thought I required a vacation. She bought me a ticket for a trip to Toronto to visit Hanna. The day of the flight came but I did not fly. I was scared that I would not make it to Toronto. I had visions that I would go crazy on the plane and would have to be restrained by passengers. They may have to inject me with a tranquilizer to keep me calm. Maybe I would jump off the plane? It was that bad.

My suicidal thoughts persisted and grew worse. They did not seem to go away! What should I do? I thought of ways of killing myself and felt that jumping off a bridge was the best and easiest alternative. I would drown and die! Simple as that! I went for counseling but that did not seem to help. The councilor warned me that I should go to Emergency if I felt the urge to kill myself. I ignored her advice. I left my mom a suicide note. I scouted several bridges and found the one I thought was high enough. The water looked pretty deep. I went to the bridge and stared at it. I thought about "ending it all" but did not feel like jumping. I came back home. While I was at the bridge, Khatie had phoned my friend Nasir and had asked him for help. When I got home, Khatie was extremely concerned and was upset at me. Nasir phoned me up and was also worried but was happy that I was safe. I reassured them both that I was fine and not to worry. But I was not well.

Marisa called and I did not want to talk to her. A part of me felt that if I hadn't met her I would not be in this predicament. I disconnected my phone number with the telephone company. I wanted to ignore her. A few days went by and I felt worse. Feelings of committing suicide began to recur again. I felt that was the only way out of this pain. I went back to the bridge again. Today I was going to do it! That was decided! At the bridge, I climbed over the protective railing. Cars passed above me. A part of me wondered what I would do if a car stopped and someone came to help. Another part of me wished someone would come and help. Maybe they have a solution to my problems. Maybe they might show me some affection, take me home and take care of me. I saw the river beneath me. Its currents looked strong. I knew there was a weir about a mile away. I would definitely drown once I hit that. In the past, many people on canoes and boats had accidentally been killed in the weir. I imagined the paramedics finding my muddy and filthy body. My mouth would be full of bugs, worms and grass and who knows what else. It wouldn't matter anyway. I would not feel anything because I would be dead! I imagined Khatie and Rozy hearing the bad news. I felt bad for them. I let go of one arm. I looked down and saw the cold, green, river beneath me. All I had to do now was to release the other arm and I would be in it. All my problems gone!

Well, that's what I thought! But, something inside of me stopped me. I looked down at the river and said no way! No way! This is not the solution! There has to be a better way! There just has to be! I grabbed hold of the railing with both arms and jumped over the railing onto solid and safe ground. As I walked to my car, I thought of my family and especially Khatie, who had been diagnosed with cancer four years ago. This would have really hurt her. I thought to myself, "It's a good thing I did not do this, I have to take care of her." But first I have to get better! Although I walked away from the bridge that fall evening, I was still depressed, unhappy and confused. First Marisa and then Khatie took me to the hospital. I was admitted. I was on drugs for about a week where all I did was sleep and eat. I noticed I was not alone in the ward at the hospital. There were many people like me.

I especially remember an Amish girl dressed in her conservative black costume, with eyeglasses and a bonnet on her head. She looked really depressed. My stress and depression was lessened as I had been taken out of my stressful environment. I tried to smile at the Amish girl but she ignored me. I was only trying to be friendly. I wasn't trying to pick her up. Fortunately, I still retained my sense of humor - what little there was of it, even in those difficult times. I thought I would love to help these depressed people out. But how can I help? Khatie and Marisa came to visit me, which cheered me up a bit. I felt real bad that I had put them through this sad situation. I apologized to them and was extremely embarrassed that this had happened to me. A friend I hadn't seen for a long time worked in the hospital and walked by. I really did not know her that well. She did not seem surprised. I was surprised to see her. She talked to me briefly. I thought "oh no, now everyone will know of my depression." My family and I will be disgraced in the community. Fortunately, she kept our meeting confidential. Later, I heard she moved to another city. Nine years later when I met her again, she did not even remember the event.

After a week, I was released from the hospital, went back to work and took a vacation a few weeks later. A friend and I went to Mexico. Before I left for Mexico, my mom gave me a "holy rope" made of white colored cloth. It was shaped like a necklace. She said it would help me in the future with any difficulties I might face. I guess it was to be my lucky charm. I could wear it on my neck or tie it around my wrist but I decided that I would put in my pocket. I wasn't sure if I wanted any more religious connections in my life. I thought about the impact of this rope. Psychologically, I suppose it would remind me not to forget God. To make sure to remember him in whatever I do. Or did it have some mystical or spiritual power I did not know about. I respected my mom a lot, so I took it with me on my vacation and it was always with me.

When I went swimming in the ocean, at the bars and discos, at dinner, it was always in my pocket. For some reason, having it with me gave me confidence I never had before. I was on the beach in the daytime and in discos at night. I sensed that I had achieved freedom from my relationship and my depressive and suicidal times. In my seven-day vacation, I slept an hour a night. Drinking alcohol was prohibited in our religion. But, I started drinking beer. It was cheap in Mexico. But more importantly, I was tired of being close-minded and restricted. I wanted freedom to explore and enjoy life. I wanted to know about myself! I was meeting and picking up women and learning and talking in Spanish. I enjoyed the sights and sounds of Puerto Vallarta. I saw the ocean again. When I was young, I went to see Hanna, who lived near the ocean. I always associated water with exploration and freedom. I felt free once again! I was really excited! I felt happy and creative. It was a wonderful experience.

After I came back from Mexico, I decided the rope gave me confidence but I did not want to rely on a physical entity to make me happy. But, I was a bit scared. If I don't use the rope, I may be depressed again. I may go back to my old unhappy self again. But in some sense it was another ritual I did not want anymore. Plus it established a religious connection and I was not sure I wanted that. In England, when I was confused and unhappy my mom had said, "go to church." Now she was giving me this rope. I associated the two events and stored the rope away. Deep down, I felt the answers lay within myself. I set an objective for myself. I will get to know myself better, know my function in this world, my purpose, my spiritual life, look into "Life, what's it about." I was tired of routine and rituals in my spiritual life. There had to be a reason for life on this earth. There has to be more to life than work, home, play, and accumulation of wealth, and family and vacations. What was it? Why was I here? I was determined to find out my place in this world! It was going to be a solitary mission, something I had to do alone, but with God's help, I was determined to do it. It was going to be difficult and challenging journey but it would be a rewarding journey. I had a good feeling about it. There was a reason why this crisis happened to me and I was going to try to find out why. I cared about people and always wanted to help people and by me looking "within myself" maybe I could help other people as well. But first, I had to know my insides. Who was I? I had to find my purpose in this life.

I gradually curtailed my church attendance and began to look elsewhere for spiritual answers. I had followed the rituals and practices of the church for many, many years. Now, I felt a strong need to investigate other avenues of spiritual thought and find some much needed peace in my life. I felt like a prisoner who had been locked up for thirty-three years and I wanted to be free, be creative and grow. But I felt guilt as well. Was I doing anything wrong? If I stopped going to church would I end up in hell? What would people think? Khatie and Rozy wondered what I was doing. Khatie tried to convince me to go back to church. But, I knew there was more to the world out there. In England, I had looked through the black and white television screen and found a whole new world. Now I was going to add color to my world. I was in search of my color television! This statement may conjure visions of escapism because television is thought of in many circles as an escape vehicle. But television can also be an educational tool. To me, my color television represented my search for realistic spiritual knowledge and more importantly, the application of it in my life. To me it meant a search for spiritual happiness. I wanted to know the real meaning of life. What is it all about?

After my suicide incident in 1991, my journey had started. My search had begun. I started reading to acquire knowledge and to get to know myself better. I read Anthony Robbins, Shirley MacLaine and Edgar Cayce among others. Cayce and MacLaine's work was extremely helpful. I read autobiographies. I read more than three hundred books, most of them spiritually in nature. Some books literally fell into my lap. I remember I was at a bookstore and was curious about suicide. A book called *A Soul's Journey* by Peter Richelieu literally fell into my lap. It had a couple of paragraphs on why suicide is wrong from a spiritual perspective. I felt happy and free and knew I was on the right path. I read many Self-development books. I analyzed a lot, asked myself questions and looked for answers. Answers produced more questions and then more answers and so on. It really stretched my mind and I was enjoying the adventure. I researched the material as best as I could. I wanted to learn very badly. It became a passion.

At lunch, after work, and on weekends I looked forward to my books and my analysis. It was an exciting period in my life and I enjoyed every minute of it. I visited many bookstores. I attended lectures by people such as Deepak Chopra and Anthony Robbins. I was so grateful that they came to my hometown. For the first few years, I rarely told anyone about my reading and learning. I figured they would not understand and would scorn me. I meditated daily with different techniques. I tried breath meditation, chakra cleansing, and third eye meditation and I prayed often for guidance. I traveled to many foreign destinations on my vacations and met many different people. I tried to become more open minded and worldly. I was out of the tunnel vision syndrome and into the light. As they say "If it doesn't kill you, it will make you stronger." I am sure it made me stronger. Problems and obstacles in life should be thought of as opportunities for change. Sometimes a paradigm shift is required in our lives. Edgar Cayce once said that we could make a stumbling block into a stepping-stone. In his book, *The Prophet*, Kahlil Gibran said, "Your pain is the breaking of the shell that encloses your understanding." Krishnamurti once said, "The ending of sorrow is the beginning of wisdom."

During this time of soul searching, I even tried to reconcile with Marisa. We got back together again but only for a short time. We spent New Year's together. After my dad died in 1994, we took a vacation together. But on the first night, we started arguing. That was no way to start a vacation! The whole vacation was ruined. After this vacation, it was obvious to both of us that we were not meant to be together. But, this time I was not about to break it off. I did that before and I did not want to hurt her again. Luckily, she realized the deficiencies in our relationship and took the initiative to break it off. I was happy she did that. In many ways, we were very different people.

After my spiritual readings, I wondered if I knew her in a previous lifetime. I probably did. Everything in life is connected. I did thank her for coming into my life in 1990. Maybe she thought otherwise. We had some good times together. If I hadn't met her, I would have never gone through my tough times. I would have missed out on my spiritual search and not achieved spiritual and mental growth. I would have never felt the happiness I do now. That event in 1991 was the turning point in my life. Little does she know that her words "If you jump off the bridge, you may be brain damaged" would resonate in my mind on that awful fall day in 1991. While watching that cold river below me, I remember thinking that I could end up "brain damaged" like my dad. I did not want that! Despite our problems, my girlfriend gave me unconditional love. It took a long time for her to say those important words "I love you." But, I know that when she said those words, she really meant it. Although I told her several times that "I loved her," I really did not know myself that well. I am not sure if I meant it. But, I did care for her a lot. Some of us have found the real meaning of love and some have not. One day I hope all of us find true love, whatever that is. I believe the answers lie somewhere in our connection to the spiritual world. I hope she forgives me for any problems I caused her. I forgave her a long time ago. I am extremely grateful she came into my life.

In June 1999, I was awakened early one morning by a phone call. I was told that my friend Nasir had committed suicide. He had jumped off the 10th floor of a building. I was shocked. I did not believe it. This was a friend that I had known for about eighteen years. He was only 37 years old. How could this have happened? I was honored to be the best man for his wedding six years ago. That is the only time in my life I had been a best man. I rushed to his condominium complex and watched in disbelief as I saw the window shattered. I looked at the ground where he may have fallen and saw specs of blood and shattered glass. Did this really happen. Maybe it did. The reality of this event started sinking in! I paid the family and his wife a visit to express my condolences and offer support. They were devastated. I hadn't seen Nasir for about four years. He was always busy. He worked 12 hours and did not have the time to meet socially. When I talked to him last, I remember telling him to call, but he never did.

Nasir was generous, loyal, and he was a great guy. He had a deep, mischievous laugh. You could hear that laugh miles away. He was very good looking. When Nasir was single, he was extremely popular with the ladies. Sometimes I used to call him "Tom Cruise" after the famous movie actor. I thought he looked a bit like Cruise and laughed a lot like him. Nasir had a smile that would brighten the whole room. While driving, he had a knack for drinking coffee with one hand, holding the steering wheel with the other hand and juggling his coffee between both hands as he changed gears on his car with the manual transmission. Nasir loved his parents a lot. He was intricately involved in the family business and his parents relied on him completely. Nasir left a big void in their lives. It will never be replaced. Although he had a sister, Nasir was the only son. I hadn't seen him for four years. Did he change in the last few years? My friends who had seen him mentioned that he looked depressed and down in the last few months. He was attending church morning and evening. Something he had never done before. Was Nasir looking for spiritual direction? His family said that he became very religious in the last few months. They found that to be positive. He started reading religious books and became a volunteer. Nasir became very active in the church. For example, he was driving seniors to church. People in my church noticed the change and assumed he was getting more spiritual.

His voyage sounded similar to mine is some ways. In 1991, when I left my mom a suicide note, she panicked and called Nasir. He was really concerned about me. He was strong mentally and I always admired that quality in him. About twelve years ago, while we were playing football, he had severely damaged his knee. He still played on and scored touchdowns hobbling on one leg. He never gave up and was brave and courageous. He loved taking risks and was the only friend who had tried bungee jumping. I admired that aspect in him and wished I could be a little bit like him. To this day, I wish he had called me when he went through his problems. I would have loved to help him out. But Nasir had a lot of pride. I don't know if he would have turned to anybody for help. He left us with more questions than answers. I miss my friend Nasir. I am sure his family misses him more. This was a tragedy that will linger in my memory forever.

My desire to commit suicide in 1991 was the best thing that happened to me in my life. It was a major turning point in my life and a catalyst for growth. It pushed me to become a better soul and a better human being. Now, I can look back and see what I would have missed if I had decided to go ahead and end my life. If I had killed myself in 1991, I would never have spent time that I did with my mom and I would not have been able to take care of her when she was ill. That was such a great and fulfilling experience. I would have not written this book. I would not have achieved my present level of personal growth or and I would not have experienced many of the beautiful things in life.

Looking back, I believe that I have retained the positive things that I learnt before 1991 but I have also been able to add the dimensions of spirituality and worldliness to my personality. By worldliness, I mean that I have become more open-minded about new ideas and concepts. As a result I have learnt more about the world around me. But, there is still more to learn. I want to know more about my soul and my relationship with God. And with God's help, I believe I will achieve my goal.

• • • • • • • • •

When did I first start to think about death? There are several times in my life when I have wondered about death. My earliest memory is of an incident that occurred when I was about eight years old. I was living in Africa. My mom and I had caught a ride with a friend and were traveling to another town to visit family. It had rained heavily and the gravel roads were muddy and slippery. The friend lost control of his Peugeot and the car flipped over. The next thing we knew, we tasted mud! Fortunately, we escaped with only bruises but I wondered about that event for a long time. My mother had said we could have died in that accident. At the time, my first thought was, "What does that mean? What is death?"

Another incident of death I remember concerned my Aunt Mariam. Before I go into the incident, I will give you a short description of Mariam and her influence on me. Mariam lived in a town called Mbeya, which was about 12 hours drive from my hometown of Iringa. But she visited us often. She had a beautiful round face and an endearing smile. Mariam was a great storyteller, and I was always totally engrossed and captivated by her religious fables. I spent hours and hours listening to her stories; I never got tired of them. I wanted more! Mariam took me to another world, which seemed so "true" that I could almost touch and feel it. I wanted to be part of this happy storybook world. Unfortunately, it also seemed so far away. One thing was for sure; I really slept well after hearing and absorbing one of Mariam's stories.

Mariam visited us many times. After she left, I missed her immensely. I longed for more of her stories and could hardly wait for her next visit. One day my mom and I went to visit my aunt in Mbeya. As I was very young, I really don't remember much about the town. I know it had a movie theatre and a church where we used to go. I remember Mariam's house, which seemed comfortable and cozy. But it seemed a bit dark inside. Unfortunately Mariam was sick and there was that word again; she was "dying." Mariam had terminal cancer. Tanzania is a third world country and at that time, in the early 1960's, palliative care in hospitals was not as good as the care by family and doctors at home. It was also expensive. As a result, Mariam's family decided to keep her home. One of the effects of the cancer was diarrhea. She was bed ridden. I remember my mom removing and cleaning the dirty bed sheets. I wondered when she going to tell me stories. That's what I wanted to know. What was happening to her? Why was she sleeping all the time? Where was she going? What's the fuss? I asked my mom, "Could we go see a movie?" I remember some people were crying and were very sad. Some of these were people were strangers and family I did not know. Khatie was strong but she looked worn out and upset. But I felt little or no emotion. I felt guilty because I was not crying. I guess I was too young to realize what was going on. I had no idea that I would not see Mariam again physically. I wondered what her "death" was about. Where would Mariam go after her death?

In 1981, when I was twenty-three, my father Hassan, who was sixty-four, went for open-heart surgery. It was a routine bypass operation. The surgery was successful. One night, after a week in the hospital, his heart stopped for seven minutes. The nurses and doctors resuscitated his heart. Any more than three minutes, brain damage occurs. He wasn't expected to live for more than a day. But he managed to live for 13 years until his death in 1994. Due to his brain damage, his life was spent in a nursing home. He could not talk or walk and we had no idea what he was feeling or thinking. He had a tray in front of him on which was displayed signs like "wife," "son," "daughter," "food" and "water". He was supposed to point at the sign when he recognized someone or required nourishment. In my time with him, I don't remember him ever pointing at any of these signs correctly. But, my family and I were thrilled and happy when we saw signs of understanding. But those times were fleeting and rare. Once I remember I was taking a picture of him. My mom, Khatie, asked him to smile and he gave us a huge smile. Was it a coincidence? Did he understand? He must have! I was pleased and hopeful.

Hassan had a catheter and he wore a diaper all of the time. He had a tube going into his stomach to give him liquid nourishment. Many times I wondered, what kind of life is this? Why did this happen? What is the point of all this? It is better to be dead than to live like this! Sometimes we saw bruises on his face and arms. Hassan was physically strong and had apparently tried to fight the nurses as they changed his diapers, inserted the catheter or an IV. Sometimes he came home in bus for the handicapped, but only for a couple of hours at a time. Khatie was a dedicated person. We were a poor family and had only one car. She took a few buses to visit him, sometimes on a daily basis. She played hymns, religious songs and music for him and tried to talk to him constantly.

In 1981, I never understood death. All I was told was that Hassan's soul would be with God when he passed away. That's what Khatie said. I could see the strength in Khatie's eyes. She was devastated but had faith in God. This helped her through this major crisis. Khatie told me to have faith that everything would be all right. She said we did not have all the answers, but there are reasons for everything. In 1981, when Hassan's heart stopped I had a major final exam coming up in a few days. This exam was 50 percent of my total score. I was not in a state of mind to take this exam. I told the instructor that I could not do it. He said a similar experience had happened to his father. He suggested that if I can, I should try to write the exam.

After this chat with him and a talk with my family, I decided I would try to write it. I studied really hard. I guess it took my mind off Hassan's situation. I did well and passed the course. I was really grateful to the instructor for the advice and encouragement during those tough times. I can still remember his kind and caring face.

In 1994, Hassan passed away. My mother was called by the nursing home. I watched as the phone rang and Khatie sat down and picked it up. She heard the news, put the phone down and said, "he is now released" and said a short prayer. She then looked up to me and said, "let's go to the nursing home." We were sad but also relieved. Relieved that the race was finally over. He had now completed his karma in this time and place and was now with God. In 1991, I had begun my spiritual search. By 1994, I had read a few spiritual books about death and looked at it from a different angle. I don't think Hassan was much of a spiritual or religious man so I wondered about his after body experience. I saw his still body at the nursing home and wondered if his soul was still earthbound or had it already gone to the spiritual realms? As his eyelids were shut, I could not see his lovely gray eyes that I admired so much. I looked around the barren and quiet hospital room and felt and saw nothing. I had questions such as was he watching us? Was his soul still in that room? Will he reincarnate and if so where? Will he come back as my son or daughter? Thoughts were racing through my mind as I viewed his lifeless body. I was not as close to Hassan as I was to Khatie so I could not feel his vibrations. I said a little prayer that Hassan's soul would find peace. I hoped his soul would find his way to the spiritual realms and find God. These kinds of situations are never easy. I looked at Khatie. Her spirituality and faith in God helped her immensely. She was a pillar of strength for the whole family during those thirteen long years.

In 1987, Khatie was diagnosed with multiple myloma, a form of bone marrow cancer. I was shocked and saddened.

This could not be happening to my mom. I would miss her if she were gone. She was largely responsible for my upbringing. I was closer to her than to any other human being. I was definitely closer to her than my dad. She was told there was no cure for this disease. This was the worst cancer in terms of pain and longevity. She needed chemotherapy and radiation. How long would she be around for? The doctors speculated that she might be around for a few years, maybe five or six. They were not sure. Each case was unique and depended on many factors including a person's attitude. My strong willed mother took this challenge in stride. It was not a big deal to her. She had seen many deaths, including the death of my aunt (the one with the great stories). She had tremendous faith in God.

But as a family, we were very, very concerned! I asked Khatie questions such as what happens after you die? What is our purpose here? What is our religion about? Where do we go after we die? She said she didn't really know. She had faith in God and that's all that mattered to her. At that time, I was heavily involved in organized religion and did not ask those deep questions about the meaning of life, death, spiritual realms, and souls and the like. I also had faith in God and I knew He would take care of her. But I was concerned about death. I did not know much about it. When I travel to an unknown destination, I map my route out and venture on to my destination. I like to know where I am going. In this case I did not know my route and did not have much idea of my destination. I was concerned, but I did not look into death at that time. In a sense I ignored it. I loved my mom's cooking so after a few months I started taking her recipes down. Who knew how long she had to live? The fact that Khatie handled the cancer situation so well made it really easy on the family. At that time when I looked at Khatie, I saw the faith she had. She was extremely brave and courageous in the face of death. If I was ever in this situation, I was hoping I could be as brave.

In 1988, I was driving home in my Honda Civic and I got involved in a car accident. A lady made an illegal left turn and I could not stop in time. So I slammed into her car. I became unconscious for a few seconds. The next thing I knew there was a stranger knocking at my window and waking me up. I noticed my car had veered into the median and missed the traffic lights by a couple of feet. It was badly damaged. Later on, I found out it was written off. I was taken to the hospital by ambulance. As I was lying with my neck strapped down in the ambulance, I noticed a lady and her five-year-old child sitting across me. They weren't injured but looked worried and a bit shaken. The lady was the one who had made the illegal turn. I was lying flat on the dolly in the ambulance but I asked caringly how they were. They gave me a one-word answer, "fine." They didn't ask me how I was. I was released from the hospital that day but was suffering from neck and back pain. In the following days, I realized that I was very lucky to be alive. Before 1988, seat belts were not mandatory in my jurisdiction. There was no such thing as air bags at that time. I never wore a seat belt before then. A few months before my accident, a seat belt law came into affect. I reluctantly and grudgingly wore the belt. That belt probably saved my life. If I hadn't worn that belt, I could have become a quadriplegic or become brain damaged like my dad. I could have died. I thought about this event carefully. Did I know anything about death? Was this a sign that I should be implementing some changes in my life?

This event really made me think about life and death. Once someone told me that these kinds of life altering events happen for a reason. So, I evaluated my life up until that point. Was I happy? Why did this happen to me? My mom always said that prayers were important. Maybe somehow her prayers had helped me. After a thorough evaluation, I came to the following conclusions: I had spirituality in my life, did I not? I was going to church every day, so I must be spiritual. I felt I was relatively happy. I

27

was thirty and was not married yet, but maybe one day soon. One of the problems I found was that I followed some rituals not only in my religious life but in my personal life as well. I figured that those weren't too bad. But, something about that did not feel right. I pretty much ignored those feelings. I had heard of concepts such as karma and other spiritual teachings but I felt my religion had all the answers. Everyone told me so. There are millions of people who follow my religion. I reasoned that they could not all be wrong. Plus, I did not see any other alternatives. After the accident, I fell back on my regular religious routine. I felt that God had saved me. It's a good thing I was going to church every day! My spirituality probably helped me. Today looking back on this event, I believe spirituality is very important. Whether it's through religion or some other form, any connection to God should be nurtured and enhanced. If you have deeper questions about your religious or spiritual practice, then it is up to you to take the initiative and do something about it. I am assuming that is the reason why you are reading this book.

In 1991, after I recovered from a desire to commit suicide, I began to change my whole life both spiritually and physically I went through a thorough evaluation and investigative process. I read books on death and other spiritual matters. I experimented with different meditations. I prayed from the heart as opposed to sitting in church for hours and expecting some miraculous change in myself. I decided to take more responsibility for my own spiritual life. I was going to look within and not leave the responsibility for the most important thing in my life — my soul and my spiritual life — to external institutions. I knew I could only connect with God through my soul. I felt that was the only path. If my soul was in good shape and I exercised it frequently, I would be a happier person physically and spiritually. As a result, perhaps I could help others be happy as well. Today, I feel I am more knowledgeable and more spiritual than ever before. As a result I was able to understand and deal with another major challenge, which appeared many years later. The challenge was the upcoming death of an angel, my mom.

There is that dastardly word again, death! Yes, it keeps appearing in my life over and over again. That's okay, the positive thing is that I would not be writing this book if Khatie hadn't given me the time to do so. Khatie's thirteen-year-battle with cancer was now coming to an end. She only had a few months to live. First, the doctor had said she would be gone by July 2000. Then the revised forecast was December 2000. The second time the doctor was right. She managed to hang on until five days before Christmas. We hadn't told her what the doctor had said, that she had only until December to live. The doctors had been wrong in the past and we figured that she might give up and lose the courage to keep fighting. But we also felt that she knew it was just a matter of time before she passed on. The doctor had told her that there was nothing that could be done for her. Her disease had become worse in the last couple of years. She was to receive palliative care and the nurses would make life as comfortable for her at home as possible.

Khatie was not stupid. She was a smart woman. I think she knew what was happening. She was making statements such as "I want to go now!" and "I don't know why God doesn't take me." "I can't handle the pain." Khatie was always an independent and strong woman. She never liked relying on anybody else for anything. People admired her strong yet humble characteristics. A few years before this illness, when she was in her early seventies, she used to mow the lawn, paint the patio, spend endless hours in the kitchen cooking this dish or that (I was well fed) and driving her Honda Civic. A year before her death, she started to lose that independence. Her diseased body could not keep up with her sharp mind and strong soul.

While she was at home, I thought that with my spiritual knowledge about death, I should talk to her about her upcoming death. I should see if she was comfortable with it. So I decided to test the waters and ask her about the topic of death. I thought that if she were interested, she would ask me more questions. I briefly described leaving the body, the tunnel experience, meeting relatives and friends and the like. I had to be careful; I did not want to scare her. She seemed interested but did not seem to care too much. Maybe she was listening to make me happy. I knew she had immense faith in God. I assumed that deep down in her soul she felt everything would be fine. She had seen many deaths in her lifetime as well. Maybe she was experienced in that area. I respected her space and did not discuss this topic with her again. If she was interested, I thought she would bring it up herself. She never did. I try not to force my spiritual viewpoints on anyone. I give certain "spiritual feelers" to my family and friends. If they are genuinely interested in a topic and are ready for a fruitful debate or discussion, I am always prepared and interested. They say knowledge is power. I could have all the knowledge in the world but do nothing with it. Therefore, I think that applying the knowledge is even more powerful than just knowledge itself. Perhaps some people such as Khatie rely on faith alone. I respect her for that. Maybe she knew something I didn't. I prefer to mix knowledge and faith. By doing that I feel that I understand the function and process of life, death and other spiritual matters a bit better. That makes me feel more comfortable.

A week before her death, Khatie was admitted to the hospital. We were there most of the time. Four days before she passed away, she called me up at home from her hospital bed. She said she felt confused and uneasy. She wanted to come home and now! She had been in the hospital many times. She always preferred staying in the hospital until she felt better. She never wanted to bother anyone at home. This request sounded a bit different and illogical. As a family, we convinced her that it was better for her to stay in the hospital for a few days longer until she got better. We felt that she had to finish her treatment. Then she could come home. She agreed and we all felt relieved. Unfortunately, she never came home again. After her death, I thought that maybe deep down in her soul she knew that she was dying and she wanted to die at home. The strange thing is that the room she died in was room number 13. She died thirteen years after she was diagnosed with cancer. My father died thirteen years after his open-heart surgery. I found that to be an interesting coincidence. Was it a coincidence at all? The spiritual world has its own laws and rules. In the physical realm, we are not really aware of all of them.

I believe that souls who are dying are aware of their surroundings. In fact their spiritual sense, which is also known as the sixth sense, is more alert before death. The soul is about to leave the body. Khatie went into a coma a day before her death. The nurses reminded us to be careful of what we said before Khatie's comatose body. We should talk outside the room. From my spiritual readings, I know that the soul can linger outside the body. When the time is right it will sever the "silver cord" and leave the body. I think a soul can read a person's intentions and feelings from this standpoint. I really don't know whether staying in the room or talking outside would have made that much difference. My niece, Sofia, was really worried that my mom would die on her birthday, the 19th of December. Her birthday would be forever ruined! She hoped and prayed that this would not happen.

Souls are aware of the feelings, requests and prayers of their relatives and friends before death. My mother passed away on the 20th of December 2000. Sofia was relieved. It was the middle of the night and a nurse was beside her when she passed on. That's the way she had wanted it. My mom did not like too much fuss. She was independent and humble in her ways. Death can be sad, but it can also be a celebration of life. My mom left us with many wonderful memories. I have taken many, many pictures to remind me in case my memory ever fails me. When I looked at my mom's body lying there in the hospital bed I knew that it was only a temporary shell. It was a physical vehicle for the soul's expression and experiences on earth. Her soul had left her body and had gone on to her next adventure. I wondered if this angel would watch over me after death as she had in done in life? I hope she will be there to welcome me when my time comes.

A couple of days before Khatie passed on; I had a feeling she would not be around for too long. She looked fragile, worn out, seemed unresponsive and was not eating much food. She was given an oxygen mask and had a Glucose IV drip to her vein on her left arm. That night I went home. But I was too wound up and could not sleep. I felt that the most important person in my life was now dying. In 1987, when she was diagnosed with cancer I thought she would be gone in a few years. She lived for thirteen years. Although you can never prepare for death of a mother, I had thirteen years to think about her death. After my crisis in 1991, I started to read obituaries. I find it comforting that people write so many good things about their relatives and friends who have passed on. They write about how full a life they have led, their travels and learning, the companionship they shared, the wonderful children they have left behind and most important, the love, God's love that they have shared with each other. I wanted a nice obituary for my mom with a picture in the paper. I knew that when she passed away, I would be involved in religious and other family events and would not have the time to write one that would make her worthy in my eyes.

But I was concerned! She was still alive and I was going to write this obituary. What if she woke up all of a sudden and was well? That would be wonderful but I felt that would be unlikely. I had a feeling this would be it. So I began. I mentioned that she had fought a courageous battle with cancer for thirteen years. Also, the fact that she left us with many memories and all of us were blessed by her presence in our lives. I mentioned about her endearing smile and her energy, humility and work ethic. The most important thing I mentioned was her tremendous faith in God. This faith had helped her through her enormous challenges in life. I mentioned all the family members that she had left behind and would miss her. She would always have a place in our hearts and thoughts. I then thanked all the palliative nurses, doctors, and the home care staff and who had helped us in the last few months of her life. Lastly, I let the people who read the obituary know that their prayers for Khatie's soul and for the family would be greatly appreciated. A couple of times during the writing I was in tears. The next day she went into a coma. When I saw her, I noticed her partially open glazed eyes and her shallow and intermittent breathing. I knew that her soul would soon pass on. The nurses said that it was just a matter of hours or at most days.

I have always found the church congregation to be extremely kind and helpful. As a group, people from the church are always there to help my family and me. They are decent people. For example, Khatie passed away at approximately 2:30 am. The people from the church who are in charge of funerals were at the hospital, promptly and courteously, at 3:00 am. That is dedication! I respect that kind of service. I still attend some social functions but do not attend church that much. When my mom passed away, I had to attend church services for several evenings. We received tremendous moral support from the people of my church. We have known many of these people for several decades. Some of these people have been friends from Africa.

Churches can also be places to socialize and meet friends. In 1991, I was extremely busy studying books on spirituality and practicing meditation. I was also frustrated and tired of religious rote, rituals and dogma. As a result, I basically stopped attending the church. I had questions such as would my friends still talk to me? After approximately 10 years of solitary spiritual study, my loyal friends still remain with me. The wonderful thing is that we have mutual respect for each other. They may not understand me but I feel they respect me. I respect them even though I may not agree with them in some areas. That is the beauty of our friendship and I appreciate that very much. Spirituality is a personal connection between God and you. I have many friends who follow their own religious or spiritual paths. That is their choice and I respect that completely.

When the philosopher Socrates was asked where he would like to be buried, he said "You will not bury me; you will bury my body. I shall be elsewhere." Plato wrote, "When death approaches a man, the mortal part of him dies but the immortal part of him departs safe and incorruptible." We as human beings have to be comfortable with death. Death is a natural part of life. We should accept that and not be uncomfortable with it. Many people block out or ignore the thought of death because it seems to be unknown and depressing. Also, many people are still young and say, "I don't worry about it, I have a long ways to go, and I will live till I am 110 or more based on new medical advances." Ask any older person and he or she will tell you how fast time goes by. Years go by and before you know it, most of us wonder what we did with our lives besides work. Throughout life, people spend so much time on other things they forget to spend time on the most important part, themselves. By themselves I mean the journey inward and the search for the meaning of life and death. Life has to be enjoyed every minute of the day. But death is a natural part of life and we all have to face it. We should get familiar with it. Luckily, more now than ever, there is literature on it. Also, people who have had near death experiences have brought valuable and comforting information back to us.

Khatie's death was a healing and learning process for the whole family. My independent mom had always given love and care to everyone throughout her life but rarely asked for any in return. This is because she had always been comfortable giving unconditional love in her own humble way and did not want to trouble other people. I guess her death was an opportunity to receive some care, love and attention from her family and friends in return. Some people die suddenly, sometimes when they are young, and we don't get a chance to say goodbye. We are surprised at how fast they have gone. They are here one minute and the next they are gone and so is a major part of our life. We need to enjoy our times with our loved ones and not take them for granted.

There should not be any fear of death, none at all! After I have discussed death with you and after you have read more about it in other books, I hope you become comfortable with it as well. The death of our close ones is not easy for us to handle. But they have to follow their own spiritual path. If they want to go, we should try not to hold them back. Sometimes we hold on to people who are dying by praying and wishing they would not leave. In the case of Khatie, she had suffered a lot. She seemed as if she wanted to go. Even if she did not want to go, her body had given up on her. She had fulfilled her karma here. We made her as comfortable as we could in the last few months of her life. We prayed for strength not only for her but also for the family. There are reasons for everything. We may not know all of them but we can try learning about our spiritual life and about death. I have tried to do that. This has made me be a better person and has helped me understand and appreciate what happens before, during and after death. As a result of this knowledge, I have felt comfortable about this normal life-altering event.

The famous English playwright, Christopher Fry, once said, "Between our birth and death we may touch understanding." In my journey, I have attempted to arrive at some understanding about life. My journey of Self-discovery has caused me to look inside and not outside for spiritual happiness. In the last 10 years, I have extensively researched spiritual topics such as birth, death, karma, meditation, reincarnation and the like. I believe that knowledge of subjects such as these can be used positively to increase the spirituality of all souls in this world and therefore increase the happiness of all of the people on Earth. My goal in writing this book is to pass this knowledge on to you, in the hope that it will help you in your search for happiness. I have summarized the key elements of this knowledge in the second half of my book. Although this part of my book primarily contains information on essential spiritual subjects, I have included some of my personal experiences as well. I hope that my personal challenges, and the knowledge that I have gained through dealing with them, will also assist you as you face the challenges in your own life and your own spiritual journey.

Section 2
Spiritual Knowledge

Ailments, Handicaps, and the Question — "Why Me?"

Much of your pain is self-chosen. It is the bitter potion by which the physician within you heals your sick self.
— Kahlil Gibran, *The Prophet*

Tragic events do not happen by chance

When children are born with a serious disease such as cancer or suffer from some other significant problem early in life, parents often wonder why. From a spiritual perspective, there are reasons why these things happen. There are no accidents in life — things don't happen by chance or coincidence. Before it is born, a soul knows that a calamity might occur during its physical life. Some spiritual writers say that everyone born on Earth has accepted what will happen to them during their lifetime — and that they agree to go through these trials before they are even born. On Earth, during their actual physical lifetime, people might not understand why a calamity has befallen them or their close ones, but there is a purpose for it. The purpose once again is spiritual growth.

Some souls are born with psychological or physical handicaps. Some parents, who have children with a handicap, consider it as part of their destiny. I would tend to agree with them. Parents of handicapped children have said that their children have given them many gifts. The children have enabled them to grow spiritually. At the same time, in caring for their children, the parents have learned many lessons. My understanding from my spiritual education is that lessons have to be learnt sometime. If they are not learnt in this lifetime, then they will have to be learnt in some other.

I believe that spirituality and a strong belief in God can help a person get through any problem no matter how huge. If I were to add the number of years that my mom and dad were sick and handicapped, it would total twenty-six years. Thirteen years for Hassan and thirteen years for Khatie. In that time, I have been to hospitals more times than I can care to remember. I have admired and gotten a renewed appreciation for the medical staff that works in these hospitals. Of all the staff, I have tremendous respect for the nurses and their aids. Does anyone really like to change a diaper on an adult? How about cleaning up after? Or witnessing death and disease eight hours a day? Sure, it's a job, but most of these nurses and their aids put their hearts and souls into their jobs.

A tragic event can present an opportunity for spiritual growth

I think it is important to remember that people can turn tragic situations into something positive. In 1995, the actor Christopher Reeve suffered spinal cord damage as a result of a horse riding accident and became a quadriplegic. Although his injury has taken its toll on him and his family, Reeve's determination to survive and find a cure for disabled people everywhere has made this superman a true hero in many people's eyes. Reeve has claimed that his accident was a random event. However, from a spiritual perspective, I don't believe that anything occurs randomly. There are reasons for everything. His condition is probably karmic in nature. I believe that Reeve is here on a journey of Self-discovery and this might involve helping other people — disabled or not — on their spiritual journeys. It is also possible that his situation is not karmic and that he has chosen this mission.

Regardless, Christopher Reeve is a tremendous example of human endurance and courage. He once remarked, "Hire the disabled; they will motivate the rest of your work force." Reeve has written an autobiography called *Still Me*, which was a best seller. He has raised millions of dollars for research on spinal cord injuries. In a discussion with television host Larry King, Reeve said, "I have never been disabled in my dreams, so my subconscious insists that I am whole, and I follow my subconscious." I believe that Reeve has not been disabled in his dreams because his soul is not bound by physical limitations and is free to roam around the spiritual world as it pleases. Reeve once said that regardless of his condition, "I am still me." Although his body is "shut down and forced to be still," inside he is still like everyone else, a soul on its own spiritual path.

To conclude, difficulties in the present life such as handicaps, diseases and other problems can be traced to past lives. Life is full of challenges for people and for their loved ones. The challenges are there for spiritual growth. It is that simple in terms of logic. The way in which a person experiences those challenges will determine their success. Everyone has free will and makes his or her own soul paths. But I believe it is important to have an ideal in life, something that people can follow when they get confused or lost. That ideal involves "knowing themselves better" and "loving God and their fellow soul." Going through a tragic life, taking care of a handicapped person, or watching a child or a loved one die of cancer or AIDS is extremely difficult but the positive side is that it provides a great service to others. Helping others makes a person loving, caring, kind, and generous. Embrace these qualities and don't shy away from them. They are spiritual qualities and they will make a person grow and become a better person.

Akashic Records

And I saw the dead, great and small, standing before the throne, and books were opened. Another book was opened which is the book of life. The dead were judged according to what they had done as recorded in the books.

— Revelation 20:12

The Akashic Records are a database of all actions — past, present and future

What are the "Akashic Records?" The Akashic Records are of a spiritual nature. They are a database of information on every soul incarnate (in the physical world) and discarnate (in the spiritual world). The Akashic Records are also known as the "Book of Life" or the "Book of Remembrance." I highly recommend a book called *Edgar Cayce on the Akashic Records* by Kevin Todeschi. In his book, Todeschi says that the records contain "every deed, word, feeling, thought and intent that has occurred at any time in the history of the world." According to him, the Akashic Records contain a history of every soul since creation.

Reputable psychics such as Edgar Cayce tap into the Akashic Records to obtain information about particular souls including their past lives. How did Cayce pick up information on past lives from the Akashic Records? In his

43

sleeplike state, Cayce would pass through several spiritual dimensions. As he went upwards through these dimensions, Cayce would see more and more light. Eventually, he would come to a place, which he called "The Hall Of Records." There, an "old man" would give him a large book or record containing an individual's past lives. Cayce would select the information that would assist the individual at this time in their life. Although Cayce's advice was practical and helpful, he was careful not to infringe on the individual's free will. Todeschi points out, that in one reading on an individual, Cayce said, "We have conditions that might have been, that are and that may be." From this reading, I assume that all of a person's choices in the past as well as all of their possibilities for the future are recorded in the Akashic Records. That is one powerful database!

One of my favorite examples of how people get information from the Akashic Records involves two incidents that happened to Shirley MacLaine. As I've mentioned elsewhere in this book, one of my favorite reads is her book, *Out on a Limb*. Before she began her spiritual search, MacLaine was involved in what was then a secret love affair with a man named "Gerry." She admitted later that "Gerry" was a pseudonym for Olaf Palme, who was then the Prime Minister of Sweden. To protect his identity, MacLaine had disguised his name and career and kept it a secret until he passed away. Before she embarked on her spiritual voyage, Gerry had told MacLaine the saying, "To get to the fruit of the tree, you have to go out on a limb." Later on in her journey, part of her spiritual investigation involved conversations with a trance channeler named Kevin Ryerson. As a channeler, Ryerson set aside his own consciousness and let entities or souls use his body to channel important spiritual information. One day, when MacLaine was having a channeling conversation with Ryerson, he mentioned the "out on a limb" quote. She was astonished when she heard this quote, because she had not mentioned it to anyone.

That was not the only time MacLaine was to hear the "out on a limb" quote. Shirley met a man named David who befriended her and acted as a guide on her spiritual journey. One day David confided in her about a beautiful girl named Mayan that he had met in Peru. Mayan had a message for MacLaine. She was supposed to write about her spiritual journey and become a teacher to the world. MacLaine was skeptical. David recognized this and said that Mayan had another message for her. Mayan had told David to tell Shirley that, "To get to the fruit of the tree, you have to go out on a limb." Not surprisingly, MacLaine was again astonished to hear that quote. First of all, it was something that her secret lover, Olaf Palme, had told her. MacLaine had told no one about the quote. She had heard it through a trance channeling session with Ryerson and then again, through Mayan. This confirmed MacLaine's belief in her spiritual journey. Where did Ryerson and Mayan receive their information about this important quote? I believe they both received their information from the same place where Edgar Cayce obtained his information, namely the Akashic Records.

Although the Akashic Records can provide insights into the past, it is more important to focus on creating a positive future

It is difficult for people, with their physical limitations here on this Earth, to comprehend that such a huge database of information such as the Akashic Records really exists. Remember that most of the time people perceive things from a physical perspective. However, once a person starts to use his or her sixth sense, also known as the psychic or soul sense, impossible concepts such as the Akashic Records seem more possible.

Sometimes, when people learn about the Akashic Records, they want to know where they came from and what they did in their past lives. They wonder whether they were famous people in the past. But I believe it is not that important to dwell on the past. What is important is for us to act in a spiritual way now and in the future. That will ensure our spiritual growth. After all, that is why we are here on Earth.

Animal Souls

A stone I died and rose again a plant. A plant I died and rose an animal: I died an animal and was born a man. Why should I fear? When was I less by dying?

— Jelaluddin Rumi

Animals, similar to people, have a spiritual aspect

Animals are wonderful companions and play an important role in many people's lives. They freely give love and friendship. The expression "love your fellow soul or neighbor" should include animals as well, right? This will be a natural progression of our spiritual awakening or awareness. Also, if we act in a spiritual way, then we will not only take care of ourselves but also the animals around us and the environment we all live in.

We share this planet with other creatures and they deserve our care, respect and understanding Animals are a huge part of our world. Most "tame" or domesticated animals don't care whether the people who look after them are rich, poor, black or green. Perhaps we can learn something from them. Pets give people unconditional love. This is a trait that some humans are sadly lacking

There is an interesting article about animal souls in the *Seattle Times* in January 1999 by Carol McGraw. The title of it is "Do pets have souls? Religious teachings vary."

McGraw tells the story of a girl named Massy who saw her 20-pound cat named Marshmallow die at the age of thirteen. When the cat lay down and breathed its last breath, Massy claimed to see a "gauzy essence lift from the cat's still body like a wisp of smoke." Massy was sure that what she saw was the cat's soul leaving the body. The article also claimed that some religions such as Islam teach that God will reward people who take care of animals here on Earth. Until I read the article, I did not know that the word for "animal" comes from the Latin "anima," which means "soul." I believe animals have souls, but they are not as evolved as human souls. While researching animal souls, I began to think about a dog and a cat that lived with our family in Africa. They have passed away. Now, I wonder where their souls are at this point in time. Are they part of a group soul? Have they been reincarnated? Did my mom and dad see them when they passed on? Was there any karma between my animals and me?

Animals exhibit a spiritual sense such as knowing when a person is about to pass over

Some people believe that pets have a spiritual sense. For example, pets seem to know when a person is about to pass away. In the fall 1996 edition of the newsletter, "Natural Paws News," writer Barbara Stein interviews Linda Madrid, a lady who claims to communicate with pets and people who have passed on. Madrid mentions her dog, Boy. At the time, her grandfather was in the hospital. One day says Madrid, Boy started "howling and looking" at her grandfather's house and was "in tears." Two days later, her grandfather passed away. Did the dog somehow sense her grandfather's upcoming death? After Madrid's grandfather passed away, Boy would often go to the house and wag his tail. She felt that her grandfather's soul was paying a visit and Boy was sensing this.

Animals can help humankind

The creatures that inhabit this earth — be they human beings or animals — are here to contribute, each in its own particular way, to the beauty and prosperity of the world.

— The Dalai Lama

I am also familiar with the concept of "group souls." The first time I was exposed to this idea was when I read *A Soul's Journey* by Peter Richelieu. This is a true story in which Acharya, an Indian mystic, visits Richelieu and takes him out of the physical world and onto the astral planes. Acharya talks of a "group" of animals having a certain number of individual animal souls. Acharya claims that these souls live a number of lives until they reach a point where the "group soul is ready to individualize as a human being." I also read an article recently about a dog in India who died of bone cancer and was cremated. He was a police dog who sniffed for bombs. Apparently in his lifetime he had saved many lives and was well known throughout India. I am sure that his contribution to his soul group was invaluable.

From my readings, I also believe that certain mammals such as dolphins have very advanced souls. Dolphins have those beautiful permanent smiles and they seem to be constantly grinning. Perhaps they know something that people don't? Perhaps they are teaching people to be happier? Many people have tried "dolphin therapy" and have found it extremely helpful. For about two decades, therapists and psychologists have stated that swimming with dolphins can help the handicapped as well as the sick — by boosting their immune systems. Some even say that dolphin sonar can actually cause human cells to heal. Dolphins seem to exude love and tend to be very kind, gentle and playful. Human history has recorded many cases of dolphins saving ship wrecked and drowning victims. Was that karma? Just as there is karma between humans, I believe there is a karmic connection between humans and animals. Therefore, just as people should treat each other with kindness, people should never be cruel to animals. Unfortunately, due to political, economic or personal reasons, animals often tend to be the victims of people's actions and negligence.

It is time to treat all animals with loving care

In his book, *Other Creations: Rediscovering the Spirituality of Animals*, Christopher Manes relates an interesting story to us. He talks of a deceased Sufi teacher, Al-Shibli, who appears to a friend in his dream. Al-Shibli relates that when he came before God, God forgave his sins and asked if he knew the reason why. The Sufi "pointed to his good works, prayers, fasting, and pilgrimages." God answered, "Do you remember when you were walking in the lanes of Baghdad and you found a small cat made weak by the cold creeping from wall to wall because of the great cold, and out of pity you took it and put it inside a fur you were wearing so as to protect it from the pains of the cold? Because of the mercy you have shown that cat I have had mercy on you."

Throughout history, the balance between spirituality and the pursuit of materialism has challenged people as souls. In this lifetime, we need to try to make this Earth a better place for future generations of humans and animals. That is our duty as temporary inhabitants of Earth. It is time to stop being selfish and greedy. In addition, when something is wrong in nature birds, fish and other animals usually become ill or die and thus they act as a warning to people, don't they? Let us heed those warnings. Animals are trying to help us. They have come here to teach us a thing or two. In the process they are learning and growing as well.

We may meet our animal friends after we pass on

There have been instances where people who have passed on meet their deceased animals in the spiritual dimensions. Richelieu in this book, *A Soul's Journey,* mentions Acharya's views on animals in the astral world. He says that animals seldom inhabit spheres higher than the third. Acharya says that in exceptional cases, a human soul does take a favorite animal to the higher sphere. He says that the higher spheres hold little interest for an animal. People and animals also become attached and can carry on their relationship in their future lives. Just as people can be reincarnated into many cultures and ethnic backgrounds, animals can also be reincarnated into different species. A dog in this life can be a cat in the next life.

Auras

To the dull mind all nature is leaden. To the illumined mind the whole world burns and sparkles with light.
— Ralph Waldo Emerson

The colors of the aura show spiritual well being

Auras are emanations of the soul. An aura emanates as light from the physical body. It is an extension of our spirit. Some psychics discuss the seven levels of the aura. Apparently, the first level is the physical and the last is the divine layer. Auras show a person's physical, mental, emotional and spiritual state at a particular time. I have to emphasize that it is only at that time. The color and intensity can change as the person changes. Sickness, love, happiness, and good and bad attitudes and emotions all show up in an aura. Even surgical operations on a body organ such as a lung show up in an aura.

Although one color usually dominates, many colors can show up in a person's aura. Greens and blues are typical colors of auras. People with green in their auras are healers and helpful people, usually doctors and nurses. People with blue auras are usually spiritual in nature and tend to be in charitable careers such as social services and the arts. Indigo and violet usually show up in the auras of spiritual seekers of all kinds. The color red predominates in the aura when a person is feeling angry or nervous or is being Self-centered. The color white is present in the auras of spiritually enlightened people. Although white is the color we should all aim for, it could take us many lifetimes to get this color. After all, as Doris Agee mentions in her book *Edgar Cayce on ESP*, "If our souls were in perfect balance, then all our color vibrations would blend and we would have an aura of pure white." Auras are most easily seen around the head and shoulders. When a person is in prayer, meditation or in an enlightened state, the aura is very bright. Some colors will dominate, such as the white or gold halo that is commonly pictured in depictions of enlightened beings such as Jesus or the Buddha. This kind of halo means that this being has a high spiritual vibration and is enlightened.

The colors in the aura can change

In her book about Edgar Cayce and ESP, Doris Agee discusses Cayce's abilities to see the colors in auras. A friend whom Cayce had known since boyhood used to love the color blue. He used to love blue ties, blue shirts and even blue socks. One day he started wearing shirts and ties with colors such as maroon and scarlet. This went on for years. At that time, he was working too hard at his job and eventually had a nervous breakdown.

Since Cayce could read auras, he initially noticed that the color red appeared in the aura of his friend as the dominant color. One of the emotions, which the color red indicates, is nervousness. After a while, Cayce also noticed that the color gray was taking over the red. This signified that his friend was becoming ill. As his friend recovered, Cayce noticed that the gray was disappearing and that the color blue was overcoming the red. Eventually the blue replaced all the red and the man recovered fully. With regard to the positive impact of colors in an aura, Cayce said, "We can draw comfort from blue, get strength from red and be happy in the laughter and sunshine of golden yellow."

A person's external choice of colors can sometimes indicate their internal state. The colors a person chooses for clothes, a house, a car or even a garden can show what his or her aura is like and how he or she feels emotionally and physically. However, I believe that a major factor is the person's Self-awareness. Therefore, someone who buys a red car is not necessarily a nervous person. It might be as simple as the person likes the color red! After all, red also indicates force, vigor, vitality, and energy. We cannot make assumptions based on a person's choice of color. Also, don't forget that auras show a person's temperament on a certain day. The next day, the aura might change.

Auras can be used to medically treat people

Practitioners of holistic medicine work with the aura to treat people and perhaps someday, traditional medical doctors might also use the information shown in the color of the aura to treat a person. However, before that happens, the traditional medical establishment needs to begin treating people from a holistic perspective.

When a person loses a limb, a "phantom effect" can exist. This means that the person feels that the limb is still present. This occurs in part because the aura is still emanating from that area. Eventually, the feeling of having a phantom limb subsides as the aura integrates into the rest of the body. When a person is about to die, the aura fades, as the soul is about to leave the body. People who have had an out of body experience or a near death experience have reported seeing the auras of doctors, nurses and family members as they left the physical body. When my mom passed away, I assumed that she would have seen the aura of the nurse who was beside her.

Auras can be photographed

Kirlian photography, which was invented by the Russian scientist S. Kirlian in 1939, takes photographs of

54

auras. This is accomplished by photographing high frequency waves or energy that emanates from living things. During his research, Kirlian cut two leaves from a plant and used his photographic invention to take pictures of the two leaves. He discovered that one leaf had a weak energy field while the other had a strong one. The reason for this was that one leaf was diseased while the other one was healthy. Every living and non-living thing has an aura.

The ability to see auras can be learned

Unless a person has the natural ability to see auras, reading auras is an art that takes practice and learning. There are techniques that are taught in courses and in books, which can help people see auras. Some people say that auras can be seen with peripheral vision. After reading about auras, I wondered if I could see one. At my house, my kitchen is painted white. Sometimes when friends or family were sitting in the kitchen against the wall, I would relax my body and mind and experiment. I would try to focus behind their heads on the white wall. Of course, they would have no idea I was doing this. Sometimes I could see a boundary of their head that was only about half an inch above their heads. What I saw was the etheric aura. This is a pale, narrow band that outlines the body and is usually no more than half an inch wide.

However, I then had another experience that gave me insight into seeing auras. An author friend of mine, Valerie, is an advanced Raja Yoga instructor. To enhance my spiritual knowledge, she recommended that I attend a basic course on Raja Yoga. I took her advice and attended the first part of the course. An instructor by the name of Amy was teaching this course and was seated in front of a red, cloth like painting, which had a yellow dot in the middle. There were a couple of yellow circles emanating from the yellow dot. It reminded me of the "tunnel" experience that many people, who have had near death experiences, have witnessed once they leave their bodies. As it was the beginner's part of the course, I already had some knowledge of the lecture and was feeling a bit bored and restless. My attention started to wander and I began to focus on the painting and specifically on the yellow dot in the middle of the painting. I tried to relax with a few silent deep breaths.

After a few minutes, I saw the circles disappear around the yellow dot. Next, I began to see what appeared to be a yellow aura above Amy's head. Some of the aura was in the shape of the boundaries of her head but some of it was not. It appeared about a foot above her head and half a foot to the side of the head. I thought, "WOW!" I was surprised and fascinated. I wasn't sure if this was an aura. Did the yellow color of the dot and circles cause the color in Amy's aura? A few days later, I spoke to Valerie and told her about my experience. She mentioned to me that the red painting could enhance a person's psychic powers. About 10 years ago when I started my spiritual search, I had taken a picture of my aura. My aura extended about a foot from the top and sides of my head and shoulders. Although it was mostly yellow in color, there were small specks of red and green in it. Amy's aura seemed close to that picture. I was curious and did further research and found out that what I saw was indeed an aura! I enjoyed the experience because I learnt something new. Life is wonderful, isn't it?

Birth

Death and birth are the vesper and matin bells that summon mankind to sleep and to rise refreshed for new advancement.
— Thomas Carlyle

The soul chooses how it will incarnate

After the soul spends time in the astral or spiritual world, the time may come for it to once again incarnate into a male or female body. How does the soul choose which body to inhabit? In deciding this, the main question the soul might consider is what it will learn from incarnating in a particular physical body. The soul might also consider what it might teach its parents. At the spiritual level, the souls of the parents and the soul of the child to be, along with advice from spirit guides, have agreed that the upcoming incarnation will provide the best learning or training ground for the parents and the "child soul." Most of the time souls will be born into families where they have shared previous lives. They continue to share lives because they have karma to work out. At times, a soul is born into an unrelated family because it has a mission to fulfill at that particular time and place. There are many reasons why a particular soul is born into a particular physical realm. In the physical dimension, all of the reasons why a particular incarnation happens at a given time are not obvious.

When does a soul enter a fetus? A soul can enter the fetus at different times. Most souls hover above the fetus in the womb and enter just before birth. Some enter the fetus a few months into the pregnancy. Sometimes, the soul might withdraw from the fetus causing a miscarriage. Or perhaps a miscarriage could occur before the soul has even entered the fetus. Why does a miscarriage occur? It could be from physical or karmic reasons. Perhaps it is not the right time for the soul to incarnate. Or perhaps it is just the karma of the parents to not have a child at that time.

A child who is a genius in a particular field probably excelled in this field in a previous lifetime

Genius is experience. Some seem to think that it is a gift or talent, but it is the fruit of long experience in many lives. Some are older souls than others, and so they know more.

— Henry Ford

Why is a child, such as the famous composer, Amadeus Mozart, born as a genius? It is probably because the child excelled in that field in a previous life. Geniuses might be blessed with a particular talent but like everyone else, they are not perfect. They also are here to learn about themselves and their relationship with God.

Each individual chooses his or her own incarnation

We are born and reborn countless number of times, and it is possible that each being has been our parent at one time or another. Therefore, it is likely that all beings in this universe have familial connections.

— The Dalai Lama

When I was young, I looked at the clouds and envisioned animals and human figures in the sky. I also tried writing poetry. As a result, I felt creative. However, communication between my parents and myself was not that good. They did not know the "real" me and I did not know them. Although they provided for me materially and physically, I think I lacked correct emotional balance. They did not really take part in my studies or understand me well. I felt alone, worthless and uncreative. I also had low Self-esteem and lacked Self-identity. But, I do not blame my parents for this because they did not know any better. They did the best they could for me. Our parents are on their own spiritual paths, are they not? I probably selected my parents before I was born. I look back on my past as a learning lesson. I don't have any regrets about that time. All the things that happened to me in my past have brought me to this place and time

From my own experience, I believe that spiritual growth is important for a child or an adult. I have noticed that if a child is brought up in a creative and a happy environment where parents take an active role, the child is on its way to becoming a good soul. However, without the proper guidance, which may include a lack of discipline, the child may go astray and have a tougher time in life. I have concluded that if I have any children, I will ensure that love, education and spirituality are primary ingredients in their upbringing. As I have mentioned, the child also comes with experiences from a previous life and that fact should be respected and nurtured. It is also important to remember that children create their own spiritual paths. Children might not follow the path that their parents have chosen. Parents are only guides and caretakers of the soul occupying the petite physical body. Most of us do not remember our previous lives, but we have all played the roles of parent and child before. The purity and strength of our souls from our spiritual paths to date determines our ability to help guide others.

Chakras

Listen to the secret sound, the real sound, which is inside you.
The one no one talks of speaks the secret sound to himself and he
is the one who has made it all.

— Kabir

Chakra is a Sanskrit word meaning "wheel"

Chakras are energy centers and are part of the soul. The word "chakra" comes from the Sanskrit language and means "wheel." As you open up each center, it spins in a circular and a high frequency motion. You can think of it as a spiritual electric fan. Chakras are also known as "gateways to the soul" or "organs of the soul." The chakras contain characteristics such as attitudes, emotions and traits that have been accumulated during past lives. In a sense these are our spiritual memories and they can contain either talents or deficiencies. In our current life, we may also pick up and store negative energy, feelings and characteristics in our chakras. The chakras might contain "problem areas," which can cause stress and unhappiness in our lives. As we grow spiritually and become more Self-aware, the overall objective is to get rid of our negative traits and enhance the positive ones.

There are seven chakras

The number seven seems to be an important number in spirituality. For example, there are seven dimensions in the astral world. Psychics tell us that there are seven layers in a human aura. There are also seven chakras. It is believed that the three lower chakras correlate to our primary needs of survival and procreation. They have a lower vibration than the higher ones. The higher chakras are concerned with love, communication and connection with the spiritual realms. Most of the chakras are located close to glands, which are important for hormonal development and for the proper functioning of the body. In our body, the chakras go from the base to the top. The top is the most spiritually enlightened chakra and, just like the top of a tree, it gets the most sunshine from the light of God.

I will briefly explain each of the chakras. Each chakra has a color associated with it. The first chakra is the root chakra, which is located at the base of the spine. This might be the most primitive chakra. It has the color red associated with it. The second chakra is located near the sexual organs. In the male it is close to the testes and in the female, the ovaries. It is important in procreation and is sometimes referred to as the "creative" chakra. It has the color orange associated with it. The third chakra is located at the solar plexus, near the stomach area. Yellow is its assigned color. When people have ulcers due to worry and stress or hold things inside, this chakra has to be cleaned out using meditation and prayer among other methods. This chakra is also called the "sensitivity chakra."

The fourth chakra is the heart chakra, which is located close to the thymus gland. This is called the "love chakra." It is where people "feel good" when they are "in love." It has the color green associated with it. Green is known in spiritual circles as a healing color. The fifth chakra is the throat chakra and it is located near the thyroid gland. It has the color blue associated with it. This chakra is close to the vocal chords. Therefore, for people with communication problems, this chakra will be blocked and will need to be cleared. This chakra is also called the "expression" chakra. As we move up the list of chakras, we are moving into more spiritual areas of the chakra system. The sixth chakra is commonly known as the "third eye" in Eastern teachings. It has the color indigo associated with it. It is located between the eyebrows at the center of the forehead. It is close to the pituitary gland and is associated with psychic vision. People from India put a colored dot on their foreheads in this area to represent this chakra. The seventh chakra is the crown chakra. It is located at the top of the head and is close to the pineal gland. It has the colors violet or white associated with it. This chakra is known as the most spiritually enlightened chakra.

The chakras can be cleansed

The chakras work together so a deficiency in one chakra can affect the whole spiritual, physical and mental being. If a person is heartbroken, they might feel pain in the "heart chakra" but the whole internal system will probably be affected as well. Ideally, to ensure correct balance and distribution of energy, it is better to cleanse all the chakras at once. However, focusing only on one problematic chakra such as the "heart chakra" will also decrease or eliminate discomfort. As an analogy, consider our motor vehicles. How do we make sure that an automobile engine is working well? We oil, grease, and tune it up them, right? We can also cleanse our chakras, just as we cleanse our automobile engines. By doing this, we make sure that all the organs of the soul are working at peak efficiency.

I have to provide a word of caution about meditating on the upper or more enlightened chakras. My journey of Self-discovery started in 1991 and that is when I started my chakra meditations. My experimentation was based on exercises in books that I had read. I was fascinated with the third eye meditation and did that for many months. One day after the meditation, I noticed what appeared to be a "burn mark" or a protrusion in the area of the sixth chakra. I always knew that I had a soul but I wanted some proof. And I took that as proof that indeed I had a soul! I am aware that our "soul light" is extremely powerful. As the years went by, I gained knowledge and became more spiritual. As a result, my connection with God increased. This resulted in a feeling of being connected with everything around me. Whenever I am involved in a spiritual activity such as meditation, reading spiritual books, or a deep spiritual discussion with my friends, I feel a tingle and sometimes a slight pain in this area of the third eye.

Based on my experiences and additional knowledge, I would advise people to learn how to meditate by taking an established course such as Transcendental Meditation or some form of yoga such as Raja Yoga. Think of learning to meditate, as you would think about learning a new skill such as downhill skiing. It is easier and more productive to take a course from a qualified instructor and learn some of the basics first. Take it one step at a time and go to the easy green runs first before venturing onto the more difficult black or mogul runs. Progress will occur but as always, patience is important.

Diet and exercise are also important for meditators. It seems that a vegetarian diet and fasting might help to cleanse the chakras. Some people have tried using herbs, candles, scents or stones in their chakra meditations. I also know people who have tried using reiki or acupuncture to cleanse out their chakras. As the chakra is cleansed, blocked negative emotions are released. This can result in either positive or negative emotions in the person who is undergoing the treatment. After this kind of experience, these people might also consider meditation on a regular basis in order to maintain a healthy spiritual and physical balance and lifestyle. At work and at home, we tend to meet and deal with people on an ongoing basis. As a result, we might pick up their negative energies. These might be stored in our chakras. Just as we wash our bodies or our clothes, we can make it a routine to cleanse their chakras. As a result, we will feel happier and more centered.

Death

Death is nothing but the continuation of life, the completion of life. The surrendering of the human body. But the heart and the soul live forever. They do not die.

— Mother Teresa

Death is a transition from one state to another

What is death? Death can be thought of as a transition. It has been described as changing clothes, simple as that. You are getting rid of your old, worn out body and taking residence in the spiritual world, which is your true home. That is where you belong.

When you leave your body, you become more aware of your spiritual shape again, the one you were born with billions of years ago, that of a soul. You may hear a rumbling in your ears. As your physical attributes such as your heart and your brain stop functioning, you will leave the physical body. You might see your body below you as you ascend to the spiritual realms. You will probably leave through the sixth or seventh (crown) chakra but it will happen so quickly that you may not notice it. You will sever your umbilical cord, the "silver cord" that attaches your spirit to your body. You will go through the tunnel experience with the light at the end. Along the way, you will meet relatives and friends whom you were close to and who have passed on. They are there to welcome you and make you feel comfortable. You will meet spirit guides who have helped you in this and other lives and you will recognize them from your dreams. Once you are into the light, you will review your life spent on earth with the being of light that has been described by many as God. An evaluation will be done of your spiritual progress so far. Also, your next incarnation may be discussed with you depending on your comfort level.

Sometimes, after you have left the body and you are traveling along the tunnel with the light at the end, you may see grotesque or scary figures, but just initially. These figures might try to influence you to join them. Ignore these souls for you will feel their unhappiness and pain. They are stuck in the lower spiritual planes. These are trapped or stubborn souls. Some have committed suicide while others have committed very harmful acts and are refusing to go to the spiritual side gracefully. They know that they have done wrong and are scared of the consequences. They will eventually go to the spiritual side because they have to go there! There is nowhere else to go. In the meantime, they are lonely and sad and might try to convince souls such as you to join them. By doing this they are taking on more "bad karma" which they will have to deal with in their next lifetime or in the spiritual world. This experience rarely happens and is nothing to worry about. This is just something to be aware of. Spirit guides are always there to help you. Plus you, your soul can sense their selfish motives and you can easily avoid them. Give them the brush off, no problem! The higher planes are where you belong.

Until your next incarnation you will stay in the astral world and learn from spirit guides and angels. Of course, God's light is everywhere because God is omniscient and omnipotent. While you are residing in the astral world, it is possible that you may also act as a spirit guide for someone on earth. It will probably be someone you have known from a past life.

We all care for our loved ones and want to make sure they are in a good place after they pass on. Be assured that they are. Death is a birth into another dimension, the astral world. This is where souls go after death. There is no time or space in the astral world. It is where a soul resides after death and interacts with learned souls or guides who help that soul, if the soul wishes to learn. We have free will and it is our choice. Most of our learning occurs on earth. In the astral world, we reside in one of seven planes depending on our spiritual maturity or level of enlightenment. The more enlightened you are, the higher you go. Souls of similar spiritual experience are grouped together. We are not the judges of our level of enlightenment. That is between you and God. Spirit guides and teachers try to teach us so that in our next incarnation, we have an easier time in our learning here on earth.

There are different levels in the astral world

The astral world is a whole book in itself. The lowest plane, the most dense and material one is close to our earth. This is for souls who are not comfortable with life after death and do not know much about it. It is a place of orientation. Souls have free will and some souls may want to stay in this dense world where they may feel more comfortable. These souls may eventually reincarnate on earth when the time is right or they may learn from souls in higher planes. Souls, who commit suicide, once they are ready to accept help, come into this first material plane. You might have wondered why people we meet on earth are so different. It is because they come from different spiritual experiences.

Communication in the spiritual or astral world is done telepathically and at a frequency much higher and faster than in the physical plane. The more advanced your soul becomes, the higher in the spiritual planes you go. Spiritual growth and not material growth moves you up the planes. After your karma on earth is complete you may have some karma to fulfill on some other planet. Some day, you will become enlightened. That is when you are truly pure and you are with God. Even after a soul achieves perfection, it may volunteer to come back to earth for a purpose or a mission.

What should you do to become comfortable with the process of death? Educate yourself about the process of death. Also meditation and prayer are critical. Meditation and prayer will connect you with God. His presence and light will bring calmness and peace into your life. This is the same light you will see when you pass on. Remember that you are and will always be a spiritual being who is living an earthly existence.

Death should not be too depressing. Sure, we will miss him or her but the person is in a better place and probably watching us and having a few laughs. After all, we are the ones still stuck in these restrictive bodies on earth while the departed ones are literally flying around in their natural astral surroundings. Who is the one crying and struggling while this is going on? I don't mean to disrespect or demean the feelings of the living or dead but am just making a point that we should try not to get too down on ourselves. In time, we will heal and carry on with our own spiritual path.

I would also like to quote a beautiful paragraph about death from one of my favorite books. It is a book by Kevin Ryerson and Stephanie Harolde called *Spirit Communication: The Soul's Path*. I read this after my father died and whenever I read it I find great comfort. I hope you do too. The quote is as follows:

"Go unto those who are dying and breathe into them the breath of life, for they are not dying, they are merely in transition. Shed not tears of mourning but tears of joy, that as you look deeply unto them and restore their human features and remove pain, they will draw their last breath and, not die, but breathe in light

and pass on to a higher plane. End suffering and misery by sharing of yourself, your deepest human resource — your spirit, your love. There is naught else you can do except to work with unconditional love."

Dreams

Trust the dreams, for in them is hidden the gate to eternity.
— Kahlil Gibran

Dreams are a place where the soul "takes stock of itself"

Dreams can be important for our spiritual and physical well being. Some of us remember our dreams, some don't, but all of us have at some time dreamt. Dreams occur in the unconscious part of our minds and seep into our conscious when we awake. The unconscious regions are regions where the soul attunes to the creative forces or God's light. Dreams are positive occurrences. In dreams, our souls are trying to resolve the conflicts that occur in our daily lives. This flushes out the problem or brings it to some resolution. Cayce defined sleep or dreams as a place where the soul takes stock of itself.

Doris Agee in her book, *Edgar Cayce on ESP*, quoted a Cayce reading that said, "Sleep is a shadow of that intermission in the Earth's experiences – that state called death." I believe that Cayce meant that the soul has the potential to leave the body and explore the spiritual realms. I remember when I was about 14 years old and living in England, I was told by a lecturer that the soul might leave the body

70

during sleep. I was told that it hovers above the body and explores other spiritual planes. I could not sleep for a few nights after that. I was waiting for my soul to leave and wanted to experience it. I decided that I would stay awake so I could see it leave!

During dreams, some people have out of body experiences in which their spirit leaves their body. Some souls have traveled as far as other planets in their dreams. It certainly gives new meaning to the saying "in your dreams!" In dreams, we can get information about the past, the present, and the future. Past lives sometimes show up in our dreams as nightmares. Remember that our souls carry the experiences of past lives as well. Sometimes these visions come in dreams and might seem unrelated to the present.

The language of dreams is symbolic

The information in dreams is often presented in symbols. Once I had a dream in which I saw a body covered by a white cloth. In my dream I wondered who the person was. As soon as I asked this question, I saw a picture above the clothed body of an acquaintance that I hadn't seen for a few years. Two weeks later, I encountered this person at a social gathering. I shook his hand politely but did not know what to say to him. I was a bit shocked. I wondered whether this person would die soon. Did I actually see his death in his dream? I wondered whether I should talk to him about my dream. However, I felt that it was best for me to say a prayer for him and leave it at that.

Presently, it has been ten months since I had that dream, and fortunately he is still alive. My dream might not really have been about this person's actual physical death. It could be that he is experiencing a drastic change in his lifestyle or personality. The old ways are dying and the new ways are becoming more prominent. The death might not be a physical death but the death of old beliefs. In other words, the language of dreams might not be literal but symbolic.

Symbols can be interpreted in many ways

Symbols in dreams can be confusing and might require analysis by the dreamer. For example, a dream about a bird flying over a body of water could have several meanings. One possible meaning might be that the dreamer is the bird and is flying to a place overseas. The bird might also represent a guide, who is showing the dreamer a new path in life. A dream about fire might mean that some kind of cleansing is required. An explosion in a dream might mean turmoil or a life altering event could be approaching the dreamer's life. Changing clothes in a dream might be interpreted as changing jobs. Dream experts believe that a snake appearing in a dream might be a sexual symbol.

Interpreting the symbols in dreams can be confusing. However, there is a reason for their occurrence. Symbols inform people; they make them think, they transform them and they bring out the creativity in them. Symbols force people to analyze their lives and apply possible solutions to their daily lives. When studying dreams, keeping a dream journal or even a tape recorder is a good idea. In this way dreamers can study the feelings, pictures, and symbols in the dreams and therefore evaluate and analyze information from the spiritual world.

Dreams can provide important information for those who are passing over

Come to me in my dreams, and then by day I shall be well again! For then the night will more than pay the hopeless longing of the day.
— Matthew Arnold

Due to my spiritual readings I know that dreams can be important to people who are dying. In the last few months of my mother's life, I frequently asked Khatie about her dreams. Once she told me that she dreamt of her deceased mother. Her deceased mother, who had died some 20 years ago, told my mom that she was waiting for her and looking forward to seeing her. My mom dreamt about many deceased relatives in the last few months of her life including my favorite uncle who had passed away about four years earlier. There is a line in a song called *In Dreams* by Roy Orbison that goes, "In dreams I walk with you, in dreams I talk to you." In their dreams, people who are dying communicate with souls close to them who have passed on from this world to the spiritual one. They usually tell the ones who are still on Earth that they are free and happy.

My niece, Natasha, was also extremely close to my mom. In Africa, when Natasha was very young, my sister Hanna sent her to our hometown so that my mom could take care of her. In essence, Khatie brought Natasha up. After Khatie passed away, Natasha seemed really worried about Khatie. A few weeks after Khatie passed away something interesting happened. I was not sure if it was a figment of my imagination, but I started seeing my mom's "image" in my mind. The image was not of a sick, bony, fragile eighty-pound woman who was in immense pain because of her cancer. The image I saw was one of a young and happy woman who told me that she was very happy where she was. She told me not to worry about her and that she was fine. The image also told me to tell Natasha that she was doing fine and not to worry her. When I conveyed the message of the image to Natasha, my niece told me of a dream she had of my mom. She said that in her dream, Khatie was in one room and she was in a different room. But they were not talking to each other. I was talking between them. I was the intermediary between the two. Natasha became mad at me saying, "Why is Maji (another name for grandma) not talking to me directly?"

Natasha's dream shocked me and made me think. Could the image that I had seen be valid? Perhaps my mom's image was not a figment of my imagination after all. Perhaps she is communicating with me. This event will stay with me for the rest of my life and possibly beyond. Sometimes, I can be skeptical and my need for proof gets the better of me. However, I believe souls who have passed on still communicate with those living on Earth. It is necessary to remain open-minded so their words of comfort can be received. Those who have passed on usually appear in the forms that they are comfortable with. Thus a seventy-nine year old like my mom might appear as if she were thirty years old. In my case the message was important, personal and positive. For the time being, I hope my niece is happy with the positive messages.

Dreams can provide insights about the well-being of others

Doris Agee relates the following case from her book *Edgar Cayce on ESP*. A person dreamt that a friend named Emmie had committed suicide. The dreamer had not been in touch with Emmie for many years. After corresponding with Emmie, Emmie mentioned to the dreamer that she had contemplated suicide but had decided not to go through with it. As you can tell, in dreams we can have access to other people's mind and soul regions. Dreams are very powerful. Although it is useful to analyze them, we should not dwell on them too much. If there is something that can be done about an event that occurs in a dream, then we should do it. Some dreams can be forceful and affect us deeply. In this case, we need to stay calm and try to solve it. Prayer and meditation can help.

Drugs and Other Short-Term "Highs"

A tree that it takes both arms to encircle grew from a tiny rootlet. A many-storied pagoda is built by placing one brick upon another brick. A journey of three thousand miles is begun by a single step.

— Lao-Tzu

The high from drugs is temporary and external

Today, at the start of the new millennium, drug use is still widespread in our world. Drugs such as cocaine, heroine, marijuana, ecstasy and even prescription drugs are available to everyone. New drugs and their hybrids seem to appear every day. Unfortunately, similar to alcohol and sex, drug addiction is a huge problem in society.

In our fast paced, materialistic and "pill popping" society, people want a quick solution for life's difficult problems. Many people use drugs when they are unhappy and have problems in their lives. They want a quick fix and an easy escape from reality. Well, they usually get it! A quick snort or a needle usually does the job. But one injection is not enough. The next time they take two because the first one did not give them the same high as before and so on. This then becomes an addiction and this kind of addiction can result in suicide and other mental and physical problems. By taking drugs, the user gives control of their spiritual self and inner happiness to an external party, a drug. This amounts to looking for solutions to problems externally rather than internally.

Many fine people such as one of my musical idols, Elvis Presley, have been lost to prescription drugs. John Belushi was a comedian who used to be a regular on *Saturday Night Live*. He was hilarious in the movies *Animal House* and *The Blues Brothers*. Belushi had a great future but died due to a heroin and cocaine overdose. Jim Morrison of the musical group, The Doors, was another person who abused drugs and alcohol, which eventually lead to his death. The last words Morrison wrote were, "I am not crazy, I am just looking for freedom." Ironically, Morrison in his poem *An American Prayer* also wrote, "Have you forgotten the keys to the kingdom?"

The British movie, *Trainspotting*, examines the problems of drug addiction. It is not a pleasant movie to watch but it had a profound impact on me. There is a powerful scene in which a baby dies due to the neglect of its parents who are drug addicts. In another scene a person locks himself in a room, goes "cold turkey" and doesn't leave his room until he gets over his addiction. However, it is only a temporary relief because he has not resolved the source of his problem. Addictions are easy to get into but hard to get out of. People who are addicted to drugs and alcohol are on a path to Self-destruction. In a sense they are committing suicide slowly.

Spirituality produces a greater "high" than drugs

I believe that all addictions — whether they are drugs, alcohol or sex — are usually associated with "not knowing thyself." When people forget spirituality in their lives, they turn to shortcuts to be happy. Drinking alcohol makes people forget their problems for a while, but only for a short while. The same goes for drugs, sex and other addictions. Sex addiction might also have the added negative dimension of control, domination or possessiveness over the other person. That is a very selfish trait.

For a short time, before my crisis in 1991, I started focusing heavily on my relationship to forget my problems. This was like an addiction. Looking back on it, due to my deteriorated mental state, I was looking for any trace of happiness and comfort I could find. It gave me temporary satisfaction but it was never permanent.

In my spiritual recovery, I have found that meditation and prayer are very helpful. To get the high from meditation took some work, patience, discipline and commitment from me. But I found that it is a better and safer alternative than pursuing external addictions. It is more work but the rewards are plentiful and longer lasting. With practice the spiritual high is achieved more quickly each time. It is also good for mental and emotional health and provides stability in both the physical and spiritual life. With prayer and meditation, I found I became more centered and my thinking processes became more creative, effective and efficient. As Morrison said, don't lose the keys to the kingdom of God. Sometimes it might seem as if the keys are lost, but God never deserts his children; He is always there for them, and the keys can always be found again.

Free Will and Pre-Destiny

It is never by chance that a soul enters any material experience; rather by choice. For, the will is the birthright, the manifested right of every soul. It is the gift of the creator, yet it is the price one pays for material expression.

— Edgar Cayce

The concept of free will is very interesting, and I have looked into it with immense curiosity and investigation. When God created us billions of years ago, He gave us a gift called free will. Free will can be defined as our ability to experience and interpret events in our physical world without any restrictions. I believe that we have been given free will to experience events and make decisions in our daily lives. In the physical world, the future is not fixed. We can use our free will to make spiritually beneficial choices and create a positive future.

In his book, *Spirit Communication: The Soul's Path*, Kevin Ryerson says, "the future is not fixed." He says, "through exercising our free will, or our ability to make choices, we have the capacity to re-create or renegotiate our future." While we are on this Earth we should think of ourselves as masters of our own destinies. With God's help a person will make the right decisions during his or her journey in the physical body. This might mean that the body might die in the first year of birth or it might last until it is one hundred years old. The quantity does not matter that much; it is the quality and purpose of the soul's existence in this lifetime that matters.

I heard a saying that, "Life is the canvas; you are the paintbrush." We can also go one step further and say that God is the painter. If you, as the paintbrush let the spirit of God work through you, you could paint a beautiful picture that will be admired the world over. All you have to do is ask. But the choice is up to you. That is your gift of free will.

The difference between pre-destiny and free will and the power of spirituality

In his book, *Spirit Communication: The Soul's Path*, Kevin Ryerson explains the difference between pre-destiny and free will as follows. He says, "Destiny isn't an event, it's how we experience the event." Ryerson gives an example where he asks us to assume that we are playing the role of Mark Anthony in a Shakespeare play. He says, "even though the lines are fixed, the characters are fixed and the event in history is fixed, it is the way you interpret the character that actually determines your perception of the moment." You can portray Anthony as a devious man, a confused individual or a brilliant politician. Ryerson says, "It all depends on how you play the character." In the same way, the people who are watching the performance are reading what they want into the character. They are observing and interpreting events using their own free will.

I believe that before we were born, in the spiritual world, we were shown the possible calamities, triumphs and choices we may make in the physical world. Kevin Todeschi in his book, *Edgar Cayce on the Akashic Records,* mentions that the records could contain possible future events. That is how psychics such as Cayce and Nostradamus could predict some of these events. In the 16th century, Nostradamus predicted world wars, the atomic bomb, and assassinations of presidents and other calamities. A person's good deeds or spirituality in the form of prayer or meditation can change a bold prediction made by a psychic. That is why a prediction on a calamity such as an earthquake occurring at a particular time in the future might not come true. We should never underestimate the power and free will of a soul.

The History of Souls

There is one spectacle grander than the sea, that is the sky; there is one spectacle grander than the sky, that is the interior of the soul.

— Victor Hugo, Les Miserables 1862

How did people as souls come into existence? How did people end up in this potpourri called life? Potpourri is defined in the dictionary as a miscellaneous collection of flowers, herbs and spices. Many people in this life have tried spices and herbs; some of them are tasty, smell good and make their taste buds light up. They have also smelt the roses and enjoyed the scent. But, when they least expected it, they ended up with a bee sting. When I started my spiritual search, I needed to understand both aspects of life — the beauty of the rose and the sting of the bee. I needed to find an answer that was logical and made sense to me. I asked many people what this potpourri called Life was all about and I received various answers from "look at the Holy Books" to "I don't know and I don't care!" Religious leaders and friends and family did not seem to have the answers to my questions. I was curious and wanted an explanation.

I skimmed through some Holy Books such as the Bible but it seemed to be a lot to read. I could not completely grasp and understand the language and the flow. I knew that all the answers to my spiritual questions were contained in Holy Books, but I was trying to find a "global solution," which would summarize details from all the scriptures taught from the beginning of time. One day I came across some books by the psychic, Edgar Cayce. His theories made a lot of sense to me. The fact that he had read the Bible sixty-seven times in his life gave him credibility in my eyes as well.

Before I explain the history of souls any further, it is important to remember that I am only providing a compressed theory of soul history. More information is available in the many books about Cayce such as *Edgar Cayce's Story of the Soul* by W.H. Church. This is a 252-page book and is highly recommended. I usually highlight the important sentences and paragraphs in my books for future reference and this book is full of yellow highlights! There are not too many white spaces in this book!

The theory is as follows: Originally, before any planets or solar systems came into existence there was and still is one God. Once a friend of mine asked me, "Where did God come from?" I do not have an answer. We have to start somewhere, and I believe that God is our starting point and eventually will be our ending destination.

People are spiritual beings living in physical bodies

God created all the planets and all the biological life that exists today. The process of creation is known in scientific circles as the "Big Bang." The "Big Bang" theory states that about 10 to 20 billion years ago, the Universe was created in a gigantic explosion. Cosmologists believe that all forms of matter and energy, as well as space and time itself, were formed at this instant. Solar systems, galaxies, stars and planets were created at that time. The Big Bang produced physical or material matter. In Holy Books such as Genesis (1:1-1:5), there are many references to creation. For example, Genesis says, "In the beginning God created the heaven and earth" and said, "Let there be light and there was light." Dr. Herbert Puryear in his book, *The Edgar Cayce Primer,* mentions what Cayce said happened after God created all of this physical matter. Cayce said that God desired to share his creation. He said God is love and how can He express love but through relationships? Cayce said that God created souls, which can be called children of God. These souls were androgynous, neither male nor female, but invisible beings of light. Inside their bodies or temples people are those souls. *I believe that we should always think of ourselves as spiritual beings living a physical existence and not as physical beings living a spiritual existence.* First and foremost, our true nature is spiritual. Sometimes people become so engrossed in the material world that they seem to forget this.

God gave His children free will

God gave souls free will, which enabled them to do whatever they pleased, as long as they followed God's laws. The laws were simple. The first law was the "law of one." This law stated that our ultimate objective was to be and remain at one with God. This means that people had to be His companions and enjoy his creation with Him. As He was our Father, we loved Him just as much as He loved us. It was absolute and unconditional love. The Bible has mentioned this by saying that people were made "in his image." The second law was that people had to love their fellow souls. Since people had free will at that time, they could literally create using their "soul minds." Using "thought forms" people could create physical extensions of themselves in the material world. People as souls began experimenting with their creative powers in the physical dimension.

Souls gradually forgot their spiritual nature when they inhabited physical bodies

According to the Cayce readings, as newly created souls, our original goal was to experience the newly created physical manifestations by moving through them and then leave the body. But our souls forgot about their spiritual nature and took permanent residence or incarnated in these physical bodies. As a result of inhabiting these bodies' souls drifted farther and farther away from their true spiritual source and became "tainted" with aspects that were not conducive to spiritual growth. This tendency to not progress spiritually but descend backwards is what is known as "sin" in today's religions. This phase in our soul history is also known as the "rebellion of souls." In the Bible, this is known as the "Fall of Man." We were souls trapped in a material existence. We forgot our true source – spirituality. Kevin Ryerson in his book, *Spirit Communication: The Soul's Path,* calls this phase "divine amnesia." As a result of this entrapment, we forgot God and our original divine nature as spiritual beings. We thought we were only physical beings and as a result nourished and nurtured the physical and neglected the spiritual. We forgot that we were children of God and belonged in the spiritual realms and not the physical. This was a mistake that would haunt us for many millions of years.

Souls had to take responsibility for returning to their true spiritual nature

The greatest adventures are experienced in the soul of man, not across oceans or deserts.

— Dagobert D. Runes

The world famous comedy team of Laurel and Hardy has said, "Here's another fine mess you've gotten me into!" As souls, we were fully responsible for creating this mess. We had to get out of this fine mess all by ourselves! Nobody was going to do it for us. God was not going to wipe the slate clean. Did we want to go back to Him? He had given us free will and it was our choice. To get back to God, we had to be become "pure souls" again. In a sense we had to go back in reverse, undo our negative actions, get in touch with our spiritual side and find God. The law of karma, or the law of cause and effect, came into being. This is known in the Bible as "What you sow, you shall reap." This means that if a person did something negative somewhere and at sometime, they would have to make amends or atone for their actions. Similarly, if someone did something positive, then that positive influence would come back to him or her in the future, creating more positivity. In order to be at one with God again, we had to burn off our bad karma or negative characteristics. To give souls the opportunity to find their true spiritual nature, which was to be with God, the process of reincarnation was created. Depending on each soul's level of growth, this process could take several thousand lifetimes. This would allow souls the opportunity to find their original spiritual nature and go back to our home, which was with God.

This process has been going on for millions of years. Even in this new millennium, people still have the free will to decide whether they want a balanced life, which contains spirituality, or whether they want a more material existence. Many people have told me that this theory makes sense, but have also asked me whether it is really true. My answer to that is "I don't know if it is true." But I believe in it. It is the most logical and realistic theory that I have come across. Also, my intuition tells me that it is true. A majority of the people in the world, especially those that follow Eastern-based teachings, believe in reincarnation. In Western civilization, we have become too entrenched in the material aspect of life. When science catches up to spirituality then we may have proof. But I am not going to wait for that because I know science will take a long time to catch up to spirituality if it ever does.

Karma

A careful inventory of all your past experiences may disclose the startling fact that everything has happened for the best.
— Law of Success

In 1981, due to the after effects of open-heart surgery, my dad suffered brain damage. I finished university at the end of 1981. A year later, my brother Ali gave my mom, Khatie, and I tickets to visit India. It was a graduation present for me, and Khatie needed a break from caring for my dad. About 100 years ago, my ancestors had moved from India to Africa. Similar to any poor immigrants, they wanted to create a happy and prosperous life for themselves and their families in a new land. We no longer had any relatives in India but we had some friends. Although India is a beautiful and vibrant country, there is a big gap there between the rich and the poor. I saw part of India that shocked me. I toured the slums of Bombay and New Delhi. There were beggars everywhere. Some women were carrying undernourished and sick babies and were begging for money. Their faces and bodies were ragged and worn out and their voices echoed with desperation! There was a broken water main and children were bathing in the puddles. There were no houses but only shacks made of aluminum. There was a stench of sewage everywhere. I started taking pictures but after a few shots, I could not take anymore. I felt really bad. I felt sorry for these people and I could not understand how they could end up that way. In 1991, after I went on my spiritual journey, I learnt about reincarnation and karma. Things then began to fall in place.

Every person who is alive today is here to fulfill some karma. From a child who is born into prosperity to a child who is born into a slum in India, everyone on Earth is fulfilling his or her karma from past lives. I really believe that. However, that does not mean that I do not have compassion for those who are suffering. Just because they are fulfilling karma from past lives, does not mean that caring and kindness should not be extended to them.

Karma refers to the spiritual law of cause and effect

As fire reduces to ashes all wood, even so, O Arjuna, does the flame of wisdom consume all karma.

— Krishna

In the Sanskrit language, karma means "action." Karma is commonly understood as the law of cause and effect. Another way to look at it is to say that for every action there is a reaction. The purpose of this law is educational in nature. The objective of karma is not one of punishment or retribution. It enables us to learn from our mistakes. Let us assume that a person physically and psychologically abuses someone. If he or she does not learn that abuse is wrong in this life, then he or she will have to learn that lesson in the next lifetime. On the other hand, if this person truly and purely learned that abuse was wrong, then that lesson would no longer have to be learned. When I say truly and purely, I am talking about deep soul changes. Who is the judge of your soul changes? That is a matter between your soul and God. It is a judgment reserved for God. Positive actions can mitigate negative actions. As a result, negative karma could be alleviated.

Grace involves forgiveness of karmic debts

What is "grace?" Lynn Elwell Sparrow in her book, *Reincarnation: Claiming Your Past, Creating Your Future,* talks about the different definitions of the Law of Grace according to Cayce. Cayce called grace "divine influence acting in man to restrain him from sin; a state of reconciliation with God; and spiritual instruction, improvement, edification." Grace comes from our love of God. It is a matter of individual choice and responsibility. Grace creates deep spiritual awakening which produces intrinsic change. The Law of Grace comes into effect when the source of your actions is from the enlightened areas of your soul. It is from the same area where you connect with God during meditations and prayer. Grace awakens the soul and forces it into positive action. Your attitudes, thoughts, emotions, motives, behaviors and actions speak volumes. No one is responsible for these attributes but you!

In the final analysis, you have to live with yourself and the consequences of your actions on a daily basis or face karma. Does that mean you watch your every move? Not necessarily. But you need to establish an ideal or a foundation. This ideal is based on loving God and your fellow souls, as well as displaying kindness, charity, compassion, peace and tolerance. This explanation deals with individual or personal karma. This is the karma that has brought you to the present point in your life. Today, as you are reading this sentence, you are a collection of good and bad experiences from your past lives. Your objective is to "burn off" the negative experiences or bad karma. Eventually after you burn it off and your slate is wiped clean, you will be at one with God.

Karma is shared by groups as well as experienced by individuals

In addition to individual karma, there is group karma. This can be defined as karma that is shared by couples, a family, a neighborhood, state, province, city, country, continent and even the Earth. For example, you and your family are here on this Earth dealing with your own individual karma as well as your karma as a group .The people in your city might be dealing with group karma on a larger scale. Perhaps these people lived together in a large city in a previous life. As a country you are also dealing with group karma on an even larger scale. A good example of group karma is the ongoing conflict between Israel and Palestine. These two groups probably have karma going back several centuries. Another example of group karma was the Cold War between the United States and Russia that started in the 1940s and ended in the 1980s. At that time, both parties had different political ideologies and were rivals.

Relations between the United States and Russia have improved since the 1940s so it is possible that the karma between these two countries has been "burnt off." The important thing to remember is that one individual can make a difference. An individual's karma affects the whole group. One person can bring a sense of truth to the whole group. Leaders such as Martin Luther King, Mahatma Gandhi and Nelson Mandela have made immense positive changes in their groups. We as individuals have a major responsibility. We have to deal with and "burn off" our own karma. In the process, we will make positive changes to the group around us. The group will get bigger and your neighbor will assist his neighbor and it causes a domino affect.

By inviting God into our lives, we can deal with karma in a positive way

To deal with karma effectively, we need to let the spirit of God come into our lives through our souls. Our mind will interpret the events and mentally act according to our free will and leave an imprint on the soul. This will replace the old negative characteristic with the good ones. As a result we will be healthier both physically and mentally.

When the soul leaves the body, it will take the good imprint of positive actions with it. If we let the spirit of God, which is love, come into our soul, then our minds and bodies will become healthier.

Looking back I sometimes wonder what karma I have to overcome in this world. After my desire to commit suicide in 1991, I decided that there was more that I had to learn in life. I went on my spiritual journey. Then I felt a need to share my findings with other people. I noticed that there was a spiritual vacuum that needed to be filled. I am open-minded and love to discuss spiritual philosophy and learn new things. I also have a very strong need to make sure that people are not treated unjustly. Is that due to some karma in my past life? Due to my desire to commit suicide, I suspect I have probably gone that route in a previous life. But I know that I am here on my soul-learning path and I am satisfied with that. I think I lost some contact with God in a previous life. My immense thirst for spiritual knowledge after 1991 meant that I needed really badly to find my purpose in life. I would not be happy until I did!

Similar to myself, there are many people, both rich and poor, who are looking for answers to "Life, what's it about?" I understand the concept of karma and grace. I don't delve into it too much because I have complete faith in God. That is the most important thing to me. I try to connect with God whenever possible and have found He is always there for me. I cannot describe in words the strength that I have found in Him. Life is a lot less stressful and easier to deal with when you have a connection with God. That connection is available to you as well! The stronger the connection, the more spiritual strength you will gain. This in turn will help you deal with and reduce any negative karmic tendencies that you may have accumulated in current and previous lives.

Marriage, Sex and Soul Mates

Spiritual partners recognize the existence of the soul, and consciously seek to further its evolution. They recognize nonphysical dynamics at work within the world of time and matter.

— Gary Zukav

Yogananda's three requirements for a happy relationship

Paramahansa Yogananda, one of the most respected Eastern mystics in the world, describes three important requirements for a successful marriage in his book, *Where There is Light*. First, he mentions the importance of soul unity. He says that "similarity of spiritual ideals and goals, implemented by a practical willingness to attain those goals by study, effort and self-discipline" is extremely critical. The next requirement he mentions is similarity of interests such as in intellectual, social and environmental matters. The third requirement is physical attraction. Yogananda mentions that this usually loses its power if the first one or the first two are not present. Yogananda mentions that the greatest thing a husband or wife can wish for a spouse is spirituality. Spiritual growth unfolds the soul, which he says, "brings out the divine qualities of understanding, patience, thoughtfulness and love." He recommends meditating together at the "family alter" where both parents and children can offer "deep devotion" to God and "unite their souls" in cosmic consciousness. Yogananda says that the more the family meditates together, the more their love will grow for each other. But he also adds that each person in a marriage requires solitude and aloneness and the other partner should try not to encroach this independence.

With regard to sex, Yogananda adds that if sex becomes the primary factor in a relationship, love may disappear completely and in its place may come "possessiveness, over-familiarity and the abuse and loss of friendship and understanding." He cautions that although love may be born out of sex, sex is not love. Yogananda says, "sex and love are as far apart as the moon and sun." He mentions that it is only when the "transmuting quality of true love is uppermost in a relationship that sex becomes a means of expressing love." Yogananda also mentions that unconditional friendship is important in a marriage. Finally, he says that it is important for partners in a relationship to learn to control their emotions. Yogananda mentions that two people who lack this control can battle worse than opponents in world wars. He says that a marriage based on high ideals, "God's inspiration" and "soul solacing charm of kind words" will create a happy and a mutually beneficial union.

Sex and spirituality

Although sex is a physical act, it stimulates the chakras or "organs of the soul." The lower chakras are especially stimulated, which has a positive impact on the whole mind, body and soul. In a sense, sex, when practiced properly, is a meditative experience as well. Tantric sex and the Kamasutra are very similar in their motives. It is a form of sexual expression that tries to awaken the chakras or energy centers so that lovers have a heightened sense of the sexual or orgasmic experience. Many positions are diagrammed and demonstrated which people have found to be helpful. However, I also know some people who are celibate and who prefer to channel or release their sexual energy by doing meditation. By doing this, they feel that they do not rely on anything external to make them internally happy. Also, they might not want to be associated with sexual lust and they also might want to reduce their attachment to their physical bodies.

Remaining true to yourself

I recently watched a television program in which the actress and philanthropist Jane Fonda was talking to Barbara Walters about her third marriage breakdown, this time to media mogul Ted Turner. She mentioned that she was "malleable" and is prone to become whatever her man wants her to be. Fonda also mentioned, "It was better to be whole again then to be a part of a half." She said that she preferred to attain growth alone rather than as part of a marriage even though she loved Turner immensely.

Life can be hard and stressful at times. But there is always a light at the end of the dark tunnel. That is God's light. God is always there to lend a helping hand and hears sincere prayers. However, if a couple lays the foundation of their married life on spiritual principles then life will be much happier.

Soul mates and twin souls

What is the difference between soul mates and twin souls? Soul mates are souls who were originally created "billions and billions of years ago." God created two soul mates to be witness to each other and to not experience aloneness. Remember, each soul is androgynous, neither male nor female. Some people in spiritual circles say that identical twins are soul mates. In our physical world, the term soul mate has been used casually and in a romantic sense to explain true love, compatibility, and companionship between two people. Twin souls are souls who have spent many previous lifetimes together. They could have been husband and wife, mother and daughter, father and son or close friends in a past life. This is a reason why it might not be healthy for people to remember their past lives. How comfortable might a husband be if he knew that his wife in this life was actually his father in a previous one? A certain amount of soul maturity and an appreciation of the concepts of reincarnation and karma is necessary to understand the relevance of these kinds of past life situations. When it comes down to it, it is better not to worry about whether a partner is a soul mate, a twin soul or some other kind relationship from a past life. Both partners are here for soul development. It might not be useful to search for a spiritual soul mate on Earth. Such a meeting will probably occur in the spiritual world. Each spiritual soul mate is on its own soul path.

The Meaning of Life

I shall be telling this with a sigh. Somewhere ages and ages hence: Two roads diverged in a wood, and I took the one less traveled by, and that has made all the difference.

— Robert Frost

Everyone has a special mission to fulfill in life

A musician must make music, an artist must paint, a poet must write, if he is to be ultimately at peace with himself.

— Abraham Maslow

Mark Thurston, in his book *Soul Purpose*, describes the characteristics of people who came to Edgar Cayce looking for the meaning of life. He says that these people probably had either "pain within the soul, dissatisfaction with the traditional values of the world, or restlessness with the familiar, comfortable situation." In my case, my suicide crisis brought pain to my soul. I became restless with my familiar, ritualistic lifestyle. After that, I became dissatisfied with traditional religious answers to my spiritual curiosity. I believe I had all three of the characteristics that Thurston mentions. These three things caused me to think deeply about my purpose here on Earth.

At one time or another we may all have wondered, "What is it all about?" To put it simply, all of us here on

Earth can think of ourselves as orphaned children in search of our spiritual Father. The meaning of life is that simple! It is to find God and to grow spiritually. And growing spiritually involves a journey of Self-discovery. In my case, my desire to commit suicide in 1991 was a catalyst that propelled me on a journey of Self-discovery. I needed to find my place in this world and to get some color into my life. I went on my search to find my color television — to find the meaning of my life. I was determined to achieve that objective and I established an "ideal" for myself to help me reach it. Herbert Puryear defines an ideal as "a motivational centre of gravity, a hub, or a core within." My ideal is to ensure that I have a strong connection with God. I also want to know more about myself, to learn new things and to help humanity in my own small way. I would like to make a difference in people's lives. I try to keep this ideal in mind as best as I can. This enables me to remain focused and it stops me from deviating into non-productive areas. As I look around my home, the hundreds of books I have about spirituality are healthy reminders for me to not forget my ideal.

Cayce says that each soul is born with a unique "mission" in life. The mission is to use the talents and abilities accumulated in this life and in previous lifetimes. If you want to grow spiritually, it might be useful for you to analyze yourself and make a list of your positive attributes. As you grow spiritually, your list will also grow. These talents and abilities are your *gift*. Each person's reason for being in this world is to recognize and nurture his or her special gift. Once you have identified your gifts, it is your duty to bring them forth and use them to help other people.

How do you find your mission? Many spiritual books say, "Know thyself as well as possible." Setting an ideal and becoming Self-aware work hand in hand. As you become more Self-aware, your ideals might change. That is due to spiritual growth. Whatever your interests, talents and strengths are, you should pursue them with all your heart and soul. You should make sure that you have a "spar-kle" in your soul – the sparkle of spirituality.

The journey of Self-discovery is a continuous process

He who knows much about others may be learned, but he who understands himself is more intelligent. He who controls others may be powerful, but he who has mastered himself is mightier still.

— Lao-Tzu

In today's demanding times, people might not have the resources — economic or otherwise — to pursue their dreams. In this fast-paced world, there is also a demand for quick, efficient and effective results. Patience and time are often at a premium. People might also find themselves leaving the decisions about their spiritual journey to external institutions. It can be easier that way, right? However, selecting the easy route might not bring them the results they want. Every person needs to work for his or her own spiritual growth and make his or her own decisions. When I was heavily involved in organized religion, I thought I knew myself very well. I was a bit proud of my ritualistic religious lifestyle. In a sense, I thought I knew it all! It took a suicidal crisis to bring me down to Earth. Nowadays, I try to be open to new experiences. I try to embrace growth and I try not to push it away. As spiritual beings, people need growth. Eventually we will be at one with God, which is where we truly belong.

Everyone can make a difference in the world

To laugh often and much; to win the respect of intelligent people and the affection of children; to earn the appreciation of honest critics and endure the betrayal of false friends; to appreciate beauty, to find the best in others; to leave the world a bit better, whether by a healthy child, a garden patch or a redeemed social

97

condition; to know even one life has breathed easier because you have lived. This is to have succeeded.

— Ralph Waldo Emerson

You should never think of yourself as a grain of sand on a beach. Instead, you should think of yourself as a "strong wave" that has immense power over the ocean of life. Every year, the movie industry honors the best and brightest in the their industry. In 2001, the winner of the "Best Picture Award" was *Gladiator*. Some of the dialogue was very interesting from a spiritual point of view. The main character, Maximus, said, "What we do in life echoes in eternity." I believe that this is true. The way we conduct our lives on Earth and what we learn here is carried forward into the spiritual world and into our future lives.

How are we going to conduct our life? Each of us has the free will to decide. Helen Keller once said, "Life is either a daring adventure or nothing." I believe that adventure produces growth. Growth produces creativity and creativity in turn produces more growth. In the journey of life, bring meaning into life by not only setting an example to others, but also by being a service to others who might not be as fortunate and privileged. How is your worth measured at the end of your life? If you leave this world a better person than when you came in, then you have done well. Did you make a difference in someone else's life? I hope each of us does that and more.

Meditation and Prayer

Only when you drink from the river of silence shall you indeed sing.

— Kahlil Gibran

Meditation and prayer are ways of connecting with God

There is a famous saying in spiritual circles about meditation and prayer: Meditation is *listening* to God and prayer is *talking* to God. People can strengthen their spiritual connection with God by using one or the other. But I recommend using both. They are both essential and they work hand in hand. Spirituality is a personal connection between a person and God. When people pray and meditate, they create spiritual vibrations between their souls and God. Any communication made with purity of heart and with good intentions will be heard

Muslims regard the Koran as God's actual words revealed to the Prophet Muhammad. In his book, *The Meaning of the Glorious Koran,* Mohammed Marmaduke Pickthall translated the *Koran.* The *Koran* says that people should pray only to God and not to intermediaries. (*Surah* III 64,79,80; *Surah* XVI 51). The Bible mentions that we should pray to only one God (Deuteronomy 13:1-4). And the Bible cautions about trusting prophets, saying that, "Many false prophets shall arise and deceive man" (Matthew 24:11).

I personally believe that people should pray to God and God alone. However, some people require something physical to which they direct their prayers; someone or something they can see, feel, touch or hear. Some people use the name of Jesus or the name of a special religious person in prayer. My mom, Khatie, used to pray to a spiritual leader and also to God. She used her free will to choose how she wanted to connect with God in her own special way. Just as I respected Khatie's way of connecting with God, I respect everyone else's spiritual practices as well. I believe that everyone will eventually connect with God in his or her own way and time.

The conscious, subconscious, and the superconscious are all aspects of our being

Before discussing meditation and prayer further, it is useful to first look at the three parts of a person: physical, mental and spiritual. Cayce referred to them as the conscious, subconscious, and the superconscious respectively. The conscious or the physical is defined as any stimuli that people can detect using our five senses. This includes things that people can see, feel, hear, smell, touch and taste. The conscious aspect of a person's being gives them their connection with the outside world. The subconscious is defined as the processes involving the mental body or the mind. The subconscious is also a place where people tend to evaluate their dreams. Also, images of past lives are displayed in this area for mental analysis and evaluation. In the subconscious, everyday occurrences and problems that happen in people's lives are analyzed and processed. The subconscious has also been defined as the intermediary between the conscious and the superconscious. The superconscious is the part of a person's being where the soul connects with God. That is why in meditation and prayer people have to transcend the conscious or physical and subconscious or

100

mental so that they can communicate clearly with God through the superconscious mind or the soul.

Even though these three areas are defined as separate aspects of a person's being, they are really not separate. The conscious, subconscious, and superconscious all work together to give a person their awareness of the universe and themselves. Even though a person might feel external sensations with their body and think with their mind, what makes the physical and mental tick? Think of the body as the car and the mind as the engine. Who is the driver? The soul is the driver.

In life, we are trying to get to know the eternal, beautiful and most valuable part of our selves, which is the soul. You might not be able to see it physically, but it resides within you. We accumulate karma during our many lifetimes. By meditation and prayer we connect with God and this process enhances our spiritual qualities, which encourages us to act in a more spiritual manner. This reduces the effect of negative past actions and encourages us to act positively, which will create positive karma for the future. In physical terms, think of God as the satellite up in the sky and yourself as the satellite dish. You want to establish a clear and strong signal to and from the satellite. That is the objective in meditation and prayer. As the signal gets stronger, you feel the unconditional love of God more strongly.

When people connect with God, they are filled with spiritual light

No man can reveal to you aught but that which already lies half asleep in the dawning of your knowledge. The teacher who walks in the shadow of the temple, among his followers, gives not of his wisdom but rather of his faith and lovingness. If he is indeed wise he does not bid you enter the house of his wisdom, but rather leads you to the threshold of your own mind.

— Kahlil Gibran

101

Jesus said, "The kingdom of God lies within you." He also said, "If your eye be single, the whole body may be full of light." By this I think He meant that once we connect with God, our physical and mental bodies, and more importantly this will fill our spiritual bodies, with His light. As a result we will be happier in our daily lives and will feel a sense of fulfillment, a feeling of finally being "at home" with ourselves. Meditation and prayer are a means to achieving this wonderful feeling of fulfillment.

What do people mean when they say, "oneness of being?" They mean to let God's spirit flow through their minds and bodies so that mind, body and soul become one with God. All of us are children of God and we all have the same spiritual energy flowing through our soul veins. We also have the free will to decide whether we will allow God's energy to enter us through our souls. This is done through meditation and prayer. Charity, kindness, generosity, patience and compassion for others are also considered ways of connecting with God. Some people believe that loving life and loving others is a way of worshipping God. Since everything was created by God, and is God, loving life is essentially loving God. Our true home is with God. If we forget Him, then we will not know ourselves well – because the essential truth of our being is spiritual. We will have difficulties in this world and probably damage or destroy our physical, mental, and spiritual bodies.

Meditation is a relaxing, peaceful and enlightening experience. I have sometimes experienced a pure feeling of ecstasy during meditation. It is as if I am a lost ship that got a glimpse of a lighthouse. And that makes me feel as if I want to get closer to the light and be at one with it, because it is my home. It is where I belong.

Many people in the world meditate or find someway of connecting to their inner self. For example, the singer Ricky Martin has said, "For me, one of the most important things is silence. Yoga is really important to me. It's amazing to find that serenity." He also said, "It's all about being happy with yourself. You just need to get in touch with your soul." Martin has sold more than 38 million albums and singles worldwide and perhaps some of his success is a result of his finding inner silence. Through meditation and prayer, people ask God day in and day out to help them, transform them, and enable them to live effectively and lovingly.

Meditation benefits the community as well. Deepak Chopra, in his many books has mentioned the affects of one particular kind of meditation, Transcendental Meditation, as taught by Maharishi Mahesh Yogi, on mankind as a whole. In Chopra's book, *Creating Health*, he cited a 1976 study conducted by a psychologist, Dr. Candace Borland. Borland discovered that when one percent of a city's population meditated, the crime rate in that city begins to decline. Borland used a group of eleven American cities in which one percent was documented as having learnt the Transcendental Meditation technique. Borland discovered a 16 percent decrease in crime rate in one year. In his research, Chopra found that when people meditate together, it increases the collective consciousness of the world around them. This reduces hostilities, violence, and the risk of war. The power of group meditation is immense and it is underrated, especially in Western society. When this positive collective consciousness is weak in society, negative trends are more evident. When it is strong, even for a limited time, positive changes occur in society.

I used to do group meditations at one time. I used to get up and be at my church at four in the morning for an hour of meditation. Sometimes, I could feel the spiritual energy in the room. This kind of energy can "lift a person up" and performing meditation in a group creates bonding among the people who are doing it. Furthermore, the people who do this can encourage each other as well. Some people find group meditations to be very fruitful while others prefer a solitary meditation. I stopped doing group meditation because I could not muster up the strength to leave home at that early hour of the morning, especially in the middle of winter. I prefer to meditate at home on my own. But to me meditation is something I do constantly whenever I get the chance. I try to tap into God's energy throughout the day and am grateful to receive it. This has really helped me attain happiness and peace inside myself. It has also helped me to function at my optimum level throughout the day. In a sense, it is similar to riding a safe spiritual wave in a stormy physical environment. Things become smoother and I get the most out of my workday. When my day goes badly, I try to take it as a learning lesson and thank God for giving me the strength to get through it and for giving me the opportunity to grow spiritually.

Meditation creates inner peace which reduces worry, stress and anxiety

In 1991, after my suicide phase, I was in the hospital for a week where I was given medication, which calmed me and gave me time to relax and think clearly. I was also diagnosed with a mild form of obsessive-compulsive disorder. Although no further medication was required I still had to reduce worry, fear and anxiety. Who was going to do it for me? I had to do it myself! I certainly did not want to end up in a mental hospital! I knew these kinds of problems were negative and would not enable me to be productive in society. I also knew it would take time and patience to resolve some of the remnants of my ritualistic religious and personal lifestyle. After all, it was the famous author, Louis L'Amour who said, "Victory is not won in miles but in inches."

What was the solution to these problems? Smiley Blanton, M.D., once said, "Anxiety is the great modern plague. But faith can cure it." I had to know myself better! Every book I read said that the answers lay within. I read many spiritual and autobiographical books and experimented with meditation and prayed a lot. I believe the answers lay in my connection to God. I could not do it alone.

I needed God's help, no doubt about that. If God would not help me I was a lost case. Lucky for me, I got a lot of help from God. Words cannot describe it. I am indebted to Him. Without His help, I would not have been able to get rid of my worries, overcome anxiety, take care of my mum, visit many beautiful places in the world, or achieve soul growth. I thank God every day for the positive changes in me and for helping me through the tough times.

In his book, *Where There is Light*, Paramahansa Yogananda said that we should receive life's experiences with "Calmness." He said that when we worry or are nervous, "there is a static" coming through our mind's radio. Yogananda explains, "God's song is the song of calmness. Calmness is the voice of God speaking to you through the radio of your soul." He said that people should keep a "secret chamber of silence" within themselves. Yogananda believes people should not "let moods, trials, battles or inharmony" enter there. He said that, in this chamber, "God will visit you." I believe Yogananda was talking about the importance of people getting in touching with their spiritual being. This is the place where I try to meet God in my meditations and in my daily prayers. In the process, I reenergize this chamber. Everyone has some stress or anxiety in their lives. Whenever I feel some anxiety, worry or stress I ask God to help me and He is usually there for me. I listen to the voice within and it guides me along in my daily spiritual and physical life. It is also important to have a positive attitude, to laugh, enjoy life and to have the support of trusting friends and family. God wants His children to be happy in this world. The way to spiritual and material happiness is to allow God's light to shine through.

I read an interesting story in a book called *Mystic Path to Cosmic Power* by Vernon Howard. He talked about two farmers who owned wells. The first farmer has a well that is dry. He gets water from rainfall and it falls accidentally and irregularly. As a result, he is insecure and apprehensive and is at the mercy of chance. The second farmer gets his water naturally and constantly from an underground stream. That farmer is relaxed and is not worried. The point of this story is that people have a true source of water, which is God. And if they remember this source, and visit it often, they will never go thirsty.

Einstein also talked about an inner source as the well-spring of his scientific genius. The brilliant scientist once said, *"The finest emotion of which we are capable is the mystic emotion. Herein lies the germ of all art and all true science."* Einstein also said, *"Every one who is seriously involved in the pursuit of science becomes convinced that a spirit is manifest in the laws of the Universe—a spirit vastly superior to that of man, and one in the face of which we with our modest powers must feel humble."*

Daily meditation brings the best results

I find that I get the best results from my meditation if I practice every day. It is a good idea to find a place that is quiet to meditate. Take some time away from the world, the children, the job, and the spouse and spend 10 or 20 minutes or as much time as possible in meditation. If possible, practice meditation in silence and at a fixed time each day. Many people prefer the early morning hours, before the start of the day. This is apparently a time when the spiritual realms are easily accessible. Furthermore earthly activity at that time is minimal and physical distractions are relatively non-existent. Some people enhance the meditative experience by using candles, aromatherapy and soothing music.

Once a higher level of meditation and Self-awareness is reached, psychic powers are increased and benefits such as "mind over body" can become more evident. Furthermore, once a meditator has felt the peace and love of the spiritual realm during meditation, no earthly feeling will match that. So in a good sense, meditators become "hooked" in a positive and natural way and want more of it. After all, it is God's love that meditators are feeling and boy, what a feeling! That is where a person's soul belongs, in the spiritual realms.

One way to meditate is by focusing on the breath

I have a simple method of meditating that I would like to share with my readers. When I meditate, I try to align my back to a wall or use a support pillow so that my back is as straight as possible. I also create a circle of energy in my body by resting my index finger on my thumb. This ensures a smooth and circular flow of energy throughout my physical body. Some people sit cross-legged (lotus pose) but my flexibility is not that great (hatha yoga or stretching exercises can help) so I keep my legs straight. People who lack flexibility or have an illness such as arthritis can use a chair with strong back support. Before meditating I say a short prayer where I ask for guidance in my meditation. Next, I start with the following breath meditation that I learnt from a book called *Everyone is Psychic* by Elizabeth Fuller. I close the left nostril with my finger. I breathe deeply through the right nostril and hold the breath for a few seconds. I then close the right nostril with my finger and exhale through the left nostril. I do this about three to five times. Then I reverse the process and breathe through the left nostril and exhale from the right nostril. Again, I do this about three to five times. If I don't feel relaxed after this exercise, I repeat the process until I feel somewhat relaxed. After the breathing exercise, I then "put my awareness on my body and try to sense any stress points in any areas such as the shoulders, arms and neck. If I feel some stress somewhere, I use a visualization technique to dissipate it. I imagine "steam" coming out of those areas and disappearing into thin air. This seems to release any excess discomfort from the stressful areas.

After this, I do a chakra cleansing and then finish off with a silent mantra session. During the silent mantra session, I mentally repeat a spiritual word such as "Aum" or any short word(s) that has spiritual significance to the meditator. Mantras and chants can enhance the spiritual vibrations between the soul and God. During the silent mantra session, I tend to drift off to a peaceful place. I feel myself "lifting" and connecting to a serene place where I sense a feeling of natural belonging. After I come out of this meditation, I feel relaxed and tranquil. I can concentrate better on my work and am calmer in my daily life. I also have a more positive attitude as well. Small things that used to bother me before don't bother me any more. Negative aspects such as frustration, anger, impatience, grudges, selfishness, and greed have all decreased, and I am a happier individual as a result. I noticed that I am also smiling more as well.

Depending on the individual, the whole process of meditation can last from fifteen minutes to an hour or more. Frustrations during meditation might occur, especially for the beginner, but hang in there. New meditators can experiment with different techniques and find the ones they like the best. As with everything else, moderation is important. A person doesn't need to spend 10 hours a day meditating or move to a cave in India to be a successful meditator. People still have responsibilities to fulfill in their daily lives.

Meditation and prayer are important pillars of spirituality and a great starting point for people in their spiritual path back to God. I would recommend the breath meditation that I use as a good starting point for beginners. Chakra meditation can also be tried later as people become more Self-aware and more experienced in their meditations. Yoga is a form of meditation and there are many courses offered in every major center of the world, so try one! Transcendental Meditation, revived by Maharishi Mahesh Yogi and taught throughout the world, is another form of meditation that people have found to be very useful. The Internet and New Age bookstores also offer information on different types of meditations. The information and guidance is available everywhere, more than ever before. It is just a matter of making the decision to do it.

Enjoying Nature can be a meditative experience

Nature is painting for us day after day, pictures of infinite beauty if only we have the eyes to see them.

— John Ruskin

Jiddu Krishnamurti was a world-renowned spiritual teacher and author who shared his message of peace and enlightenment with people all over the world for more than fifty years of his life. To add a twist to the concept of meditation, he said that meditation can occur if you are sitting on a bus or walking on the beach or listening to birds sing or even looking at the face of a child or your wife or husband. Could it be a case of daydreaming? That is possible but I don't agree. When my mom was dying, due to a long and courageous battle with cancer, I was feeling a bit stressed out. Since I live only an hour away from the Canadian Rocky Mountains, I drove there to get a break. Nature really helped me out. I began to think of the mountains, the rivers, the lakes, the pine trees and the deer and the elk — basically the whole of Nature — to be a meditation in itself. As I left the city and caught the first glimpse of the mountains and smelt the fresh air, I could feel the release of tension from my shoulders. My mind became clear and my concentration increased. I left my stresses behind and in a sense used Nature not only as a dumping ground for my problems but also a source of reflection and contemplation.

Most of the time, the radio in my car is switched off. Barbara De Angelis, Ph.D., in her book *Real Moments*, calls cars "moving meditation centers." Once I drove for about 60 kilometers without remembering too much about the trip. I just absorbed Nature or God's energy as I drove. I came back from my short trip invigorated and ready to tackle the following week's problems. To me that was a form of meditation and it helped me a great deal in those difficult times.

Prayer is also a way of connecting with God

Everything begins with prayer, spending a little time on our knees .... If all the world's rulers and leaders would spend a little time on their knees before God, I believe we would have a better world.
— Mother Teresa

Prayers are high frequency vibrations that connect a person with God. I believe that saying prayers is beneficial both in good times and bad. Sometimes spirituality is forgotten in good times. Sometimes people say, "I have prayed and prayed but no one hears me." I don't think that that is true at all. God hears all prayers and things happen for a reason. A person's karma plays an important role. Everyone on Earth is here to learn in some way or another. All we can do is pray, work hard and hope for the best. It is not useful to blame God or anybody else. I believe prayer needs to be unconditional and the motive good and pure. Prayers are also important for a person who is sick or dying. My family always prayed for Khatie, especially in the last few months of her life. A person, who has completed their function in this world, will leave his or her body and go on to the next learning experience. *The Tibetan Book of the Dead* as well as other Holy Books has emphasized the fact that prayers are important for people who are dying. It eases their transition to the next phase of their spiritual journey.

Prayers can be said individually or in a group. In some churches, prayers are said in languages that a person may not completely comprehend. If the prayer is in a different language or if it is not comprehensible, try to find out what is being said. In that way, a person can pray correctly and not blindly. I believe it is better for a person to say a short prayer that they understand than to say a long one, either in a group setting or alone that is incomprehensible to them. In addition, I believe that, whether a person goes to church or not, it is most beneficial to pray with the heart. Prayer creates a personal contact between the person who is praying and God and nothing else can touch that. It is a special and unique connection.

Prayers can help people who are sick

A candle is a small thing. But one candle can light another. And as it gives its flames to the other, see how its own light increases! Light is the power to dispel darkness. You have this power to move back the darkness in yourself and in others with the birth of light created when one mind illuminates another, when one heart kindles another, when one man strengthens another. And its flame also enlarges within you as you pass it on.

— The Eternal Light

In the book *The Faith Factor,* authors Dale A. Matthews M.D. and Connie Clark discuss a study done at the San Francisco General Hospital by Randolph Byrd, M.D. Matthews describes this 1988 study as the "the most famous and provocative scientific prayer study to date." This study tried to clinically measure the effects of intercessory prayer. Two groups were randomly picked. None of the patients knew which group they belonged to. One group of 192 patients was prayed for by outside intercessors ("born-again" Christians from around the country). They were informed of the patients' names and clinical status. They committed to pray regularly until the patients were discharged from the hospital. The second group was the control group, which consisted of 201 patients who were not given any kind of prayer. While the patients were hospitalized, Dr. Byrd measured multiple clinical variables and complications of the illnesses. The presence of higher numbers of variables indicated more severe illness and/or

111

complications. Byrd found that patients in the control group were nearly twice as likely to suffer complications than were patients in the prayer group. As this study proves, prayers can help people who are ill or are suffering.

To end this section on meditation and prayer, I would like to share the following inspirational poem by Mary Stevenson called *Footprints in the Sand*. I find this poem to be very heartwarming. In 1936, 14-year-old Mary wrote this poem saying that God gave her the words while she just pushed the pencil. In the 1960s Mary sent the poem as well as some cookies to soldiers in Vietnam with a desire to give them spiritual strength. Mary passed away in 1999. The poem is as follows:

One night a man had a dream. He dreamed he was walking along the beach with the Lord. Across the sky flashed scenes from his life. For each scene he noticed two sets of footprints in the sand: one belonging to him, and the other to the Lord. When the last scene of his life flashed before him, he looked back at the footprints in the sand. He noticed that many times along the path of his life there was only one set of footprints. He also noticed that it happened at the very lowest and saddest times in his life. This really bothered him and he questioned the Lord about it: "Lord, you said that once I decided to follow you, you'd walk with me all the way. But I have noticed that during the most troublesome times in my life, there is only one set of footprints. I don't understand why when I needed you most you would leave me." The Lord replied: "My son, my precious child, I love you and I would never leave you. During your times of trial and suffering, when you see only one set of footprints, it was then that I carried you."

Mentors

When the student is ready, the teacher will appear.
— Indian proverb

After my crisis in 1991, I was ready for a teacher to appear. Because of my strict religious upbringing, I was tired of so called "religious people" who dogmatically told me to "do this or that," but often had no satisfactory answers to my spiritual questions. I had an immense thirst to learn the "how" and "why" of everything. As I began my voyage of Self-discovery, I began to eagerly consume hundreds of books about spirituality. The writers of these books have become my mentors. Without them, I would not have been able to enhance my spiritual knowledge. Some writers have had more impact on me than others. Anthony Robbins taught me to live with passion. Krishnamurti taught me to be an observer, an investigator, and an analyst of souls and of human nature. Paramahansa Yogananda taught me about the gentleness and wisdom of spirituality. Dr. Raymond Moody exposed me to people who have had near death experiences. Deepak Chopra taught me about the relationship between mind and body. The subtle spiritual poetry of Kahlil Gibran as well as that of Jelaluddin Rumi touched my heart and soul. As a trance channeler, Kevin Ryerson and his entities communicated much needed spiritual knowledge and wisdom. His book, *Spirit*

Communication: The Soul's Path, is one of my favorite books. I have read it so many times that I have practically worn it out! The section on death is one that I have referred to over and over again in my soul's journey.

Aside from these writers, two of my primary mentors are Shirley MacLaine and Edgar Cayce. In the early 90s, after reading her book *Out on a Limb,* I also wanted to go on my own voyage of Self-discovery. I could relate to her search for the meaning of life. She exposed me to a spiritual and psychic world that I desperately yearned for. She talked about God, souls, past lives, spirit guides, mind over body, UFOs and the like. I was totally engrossed with her experiences and knowledge. Edgar Cayce has had a major impact on me as well. He was exceptional. He gave some 14,000 readings throughout his life. Many authors have written on his work and his biography, *There is a River: The Story of Edgar Cayce,* by Thomas Sugrue is an excellent and worthwhile read. Cayce was known as the "sleeping prophet" because he gave readings while in a trance. Cayce's spiritual readings on reincarnation, karma, soul development, the meaning of life, meditation and other spiritual teachings have been extremely helpful and valuable to my education and soul growth. Although he was brought up in a Christian environment, Cayce's teachings were based on both Eastern and Western belief systems. When he gave his spiritual readings, they applied to all people regardless of their religions. That was the beauty in his readings — the message of the oneness of all souls, or as he called it "the law of one."

Cayce said that it is very important to gain spiritual knowledge. But, he also said that what is more important is what people do with that knowledge. He was concerned with the application of knowledge. How would a person apply spiritual principles to their daily lives? How do they treat the people around them? What motives and attitudes are behind their actions? Similar to eastern philosophers, Cayce stressed that the answers lay within each person.

Each person has to know himself or herself in order to know God. He stressed that meaningful changes in people occur in the deepest levels of the soul.

Mind over body

The intuitive mind is a sacred gift and the rational mind is a faithful servant. We have created a society that honors the servant and has forgotten the gift.

— Albert Einstein

The mind can help heal the body

Edgar Cayce said that, "The spirit is the life, the mind is the builder, and the physical is the result." The spirit is God's spirit. The mind is the mind of the soul. The body is the physical body and the brain. All aspects of a person's being are interconnected. If people are constantly under stress, their minds will trigger chemicals in their bodies, which can eventually cause diseases to arise. I have heard that people who keep their feelings to themselves; especially feelings of the heart, are more prone to heart disease. My dad, Hassan, kept a lot of emotions inside of himself. I am sure that contributed to his blocked arteries. And if a person holds feelings inside in this life and has heart problems as a result, then they might carry that with them into their next life. I have no doubt that problems with a person's "insides" or soul will affect their physical and psychological well being. The mind has immense power over the body – both negative and positive.

According to a study conducted by Dr. John H. Sinard, as reported in *The Journal of the American Medical Association*, patients might have decided to postpone dying until after the New Year to see how the year 2000 turned out. He compared the month-to-month death rates at his Connecticut hospital since 1997. Sinard found a conspicuously high rate for January 2000. While the rates hovered around 75 for most months, there were 123 deaths in January 2000. Sinard credits the "will to live" for keeping at least some patients alive into the next century. He notes that the "will to live" has often been disregarded as nonscientific. But Sinard said, "Data suggests a role for the patient's state of mind in postponing his or her own outcome." To me, this is another example of mind over body.

My mom, Khatie, had cancer for thirteen years. She had immense faith in God. Although she was on morphine because of the pain, she was still mentally alert. She handled pain very well. She had a tremendous desire to be independent. She wanted to live a normal life and her will power was incredible. She refused wheelchairs and always wanted to walk. She did not want to be a burden on her family. She would leave her bedroom with both hands on her four-wheeled dark blue walker. She would make a right turn and enter the living room. She would walk around the coffee table and couches. Next she would enter the kitchen and maneuver around the kitchen table. She would go back to the living room and start the circle again. Sometimes she would do this several times a day. She had a fierce determination to make her life better. Could this be mind over body? I would think so. We should never underestimate the power of the mind of the soul. I had first hand proof of that while witnessing the difficult life of my mom.

Pete A. Sanders mentioned an interesting case in his book, *You are Psychic*. Sanders is an M.I.T graduate in biomedical chemistry and brain science. He discusses a lady named Emily who had a mammogram. It revealed a "nickel sized lump in her right breast." Due to the tumor, Emily's doctors advised her to do a biopsy to see if the tumor was malignant. If it were malignant, a mastectomy would be necessary. Because of other urgent matters, she could only do a biopsy after two weeks. Emily was a student of the "Free Soul Course" taught by Sanders and had learned the techniques of Self-healing. She decided to use the two weeks before the biopsy to try to reduce the size of the tumor or possibly remove it completely. During the two weeks, many times a day, Emily let her mind travel to the growth in her breast. She visualized withdrawing energy from the tumor. Emily mentally ordered her white blood cells and immune system to attack the tumor, break it down and carry it away. Then she imagined the cells near the tumor growing normally and creating new, normal cells where the tumor had been.

Emily decided that she was not going to allow the cancer to beat her like it did her dad. She doubled and redoubled her efforts at doing this exercise. When Emily performed this exercise she sensed heat and a bit of pain at the site of the tumor. At breakfast, lunch, dinner and bedtime and whenever Emily got the chance, she mentally attacked her tumor. Her effort involved sheer willpower, determination, commitment and faith. After two weeks, the doctors could not find the tumor. It had disappeared. The doctors were surprised and shocked. I have heard of many cases such as this. A word of warning: when doing these exercises, I believe a person should be hopeful and positive but not raise their expectations to a point where they come crashing down if things don't work out. After all, there are other factors such as karma that influence a person's life. It is important to be realistic, levelheaded, and to have faith in God.

When dealing with issues such as mind over body, it is wise to remember spirituality. Imagine that a person falls into a huge dark hole in the ground. The hole is two hundred feet deep. The person tries to climb up but can't get out. The person needs a ladder. God is that ladder. The ladder will take the person up into the light. Everyone needs to spend some time alone to allow the power of God's spirit to come into him or her. This will increase Self-awareness, which is key in mind over body. Also, don't forget to enjoy life — laughter is definitely the best medicine. And guess what? It doesn't require a prescription, and it's free of charge!

When someone is ill, the whole person needs to be treated, not just the body

The cure of many diseases is unknown to the physicians of Hellas, because they are ignorant of the whole, which ought to be studied also; for the part can never be well unless the whole is well.... This is the great error of our day in the treatment of the human body, that the physicians separate the soul from the body.
— Plato, Greek Philosopher

Sometimes, medical doctors take care of symptoms and do not look seriously enough at the source of the problem. At times, doctors use surgery as the quick cure for a problem. I respect doctors but I think they need to become more holistic in their approach. They have to look at the individual as a whole — composed of mind, body and soul — and not just a body. People are using more natural supplements such as garlic and vitamins these days. I notice that some traditional doctors are on the defensive because they do not understand the value and effectiveness of traditional medicines. In the last year before Khatie's death, I noticed that the doctors had lost hope and could do no more. Her mind was sharp but her body had had enough. The medical doctors could not help her any more and I felt they had lost the human touch. In medical school, doctors take an oath to treat their patients and keep them alive. When they cannot do this any more, I suspect they might feel helpless and this might result in them appearing as uncaring. It might be a defense mechanism. That is why I like the holistic approach. This does not put additional pressure on doctors and it makes them understand that patients are more than just a body. They also have a soul.

Since I was a young child in Africa I have had a bad case of asthma. Later on in life, I noticed that stress makes it worse. The doctors gave me medications that helped with the symptoms. I took inhalers for a long time until I was in my early thirties. When I started to meditate, my stress level went down and the symptoms of my asthma were also greatly reduced. Now I rarely use inhalers. If I hadn't made positive changes such as starting to meditate, I would still be taking steroids, which have many negative side effects such as damaging bones. I have a cousin, Mina, who has been taking steroids for her asthma for many years. She is only in her late thirties. I suggested to her many times to meditate and try alternative medicines and naturopathy to reduce her stresses and decrease her asthma. Unfortunately, Mina did not take this advice. A few years ago, she had an artificial hip implanted into her body. I believe this was a result of the medications that she has been taking. In my case, did a doctor tell me to meditate? Of course not! As I have said, most doctors are trained to help bodies and not souls. Wouldn't it be great if people could cure themselves? Once people become more spiritual, they might be able to do more of that. In the meantime, it is important for a person to look for the source of their medical problems. The symptoms can be turned off temporarily with steroids and other medications that might have harmful side effects. But the symptoms might grow into bigger problems later on. So I believe it is better to find the source of the problem and deal with it now.

Changes in lifestyle also help in healing

Correct diet and exercise are also important for the mind, body and soul and should not be forgotten. More vegetables, fruit and fiber in the diet will often be helpful. Many people have switched to a vegetarian diet and found it beneficial as well. Alternative therapies such as Reiki, Tai Chi, acupuncture and the like have become popular in the past few years. This is certainly understandable: After all, this is the New Age, which is the relearning of ancient wisdom. I have also found books such as *Quantum Healing* by Deepak Chopra to be very useful in the areas of mind over body medicine and Ayurvedic healing. Also, I find books on psychic healing to be very useful. Naturopaths, who use holistic ways of healing, have helped many people as well.

Near Death and Out of Body Experiences

If you could take the human heart and listen to it, it would be like listening to a seashell. You would hear in it the hollow murmur of the infinite ocean to which it belongs, from which it draws its profoundest inspiration, and for which it yearns.

— Edwin Hubbell Chapin

People report similar Near Death Experiences

Many people have had Near Death Experiences (NDEs). Dr Raymond Moody has spent more than 20 years studying this area and has written several books on this topic. He has talked to many people who have had this experience. Dr. Moody mentions in one of his books that the pollster George Gallup found that eight million people in the United States have had a near death experience. Dr. Melvin Morse, a pediatrician, has studied near death experiences in children. Near death experiences occur when a person is "dead" for a few seconds or minutes of physical time. The person then comes back to his body and remembers the "after death" experience. The most common experience of near death that people have is summarized as follows. As the person is pronounced dead, he or she hears a rumbling sound in his ears and then goes through a dark tunnel, which has a light at the end of it. There the person meets a "being of light" whom some refer to as God. This being of light usually gives the person a choice to go back to earth or to stay. Sometimes, there is no choice. The person has to go back to the body because it is not time for this soul to leave the body permanently yet. The soul may still have more karma to fulfill in the physical world.

The famous psychoanalyst Carl Jung had a near death experience. He was asked to go back and finish his work. After the near death experience, he felt his life on earth was a prison and he did not want to leave the spiritual world. Peter Sellers, known for his world famous Inspector Clouseau character and one of the funniest actors I have ever seen, has also had a near death experience, which Shirley MacLaine relates in her book, *Out on a Limb*. The doctor had cut into Peter Seller's chest and was massaging his heart. Sellers saw all of this from outside his body. He then proceeded towards this kind, loving and "beautiful light." The doctor refused to give up on Sellers even though there was no pulse. Peter Sellers saw a hand come out of the light to pull him in. At that point, the doctor started Seller's heart and the voice attached to the hand told Sellers that it was not his time yet. He was told that he still had things to finish on earth. Sellers said that he was "bitterly disappointed" about coming back to the body. Sellers had not confided in many people about his experience because he thought he might be ridiculed. One and a half years after this incident, Peter Sellers completed his karma on earth and passed on.

People often become spiritually transformed after a Near Death Experience

People who have near death experiences generally change their lives for the positive. Most of them go through major transformations. People who attempt to commit suicide and have a near death experience come back as better people who know that suicide is very wrong. Before a near death experience, some people had a fear of dying or did not know much about it. After their experience, they have no fear of dying at all! They see the importance of love in their lives, they sense that everything in this world is connected, and they want to grow and learn and become better human beings. People who have had this experience also tend to develop more of their spiritual side because they realize that they are spiritual beings living an earthly existence. Dr. Raymond Moody has studied people from all sorts of religious backgrounds who have had near death experiences. In his book, *The Light Beyond*, Moody mentions that people who have had near death experiences claim, "religion concerns your ability to love - not doctrines and denominations." Dr. Kenneth Ring, who has also studied near death experiences, mentions that love and knowledge are important things in life and that formal religions have added dogma and doctrine. In one of Moody's studies, an elderly and a very religious woman was a doctrine abiding Lutheran before her near death experience. After the experience, she mentioned that God "didn't care about church doctrine at all."

Scientific study proves the existence of a "functioning mind" after death

I saw an interesting interview on the Discovery channel with Dr. Sam Parnia, a clinical neuroscientist in Hastings, England. Dr. Parnia conducted a study on people who had a near death experience. His study included people whose hearts had stopped and had no brain activity. Dr. Parnia said that their "brain waves had gone flat." Dr. Parnia described his patients as having "lucid, well-structured, memory" of the events after their brains had stopped working. The brain was dead. It was as if "there was a functioning mind when the brain stops working" as the doctor put it. Even though the doctor was talking from a scientific viewpoint, spiritualists will tell you that the patient's soul had left the body. The functioning mind was the soul. Once the soul came back into the body, it left its memory imprint on the brain. The BBC News service in October 2000 also reported this same study in their Internet article *Evidence of "Life After Death."* They reported that patients in Parnia's study "told of feelings of peace and joy, time speeded up, heightened senses, lost awareness of body, seeing a bright light, entering another world, encountering a mystical being and coming to a point of no return." The BBC reported that none of the patients were found to have low oxygen levels — which some scientists believe may be responsible for so-called "near-death" experiences. Near death experiences are normal. There is nothing to fear; the soul is eternal.

People can have both a near death and an out of body experience

My mom, Khatie, had both a near death and an out of body experience. About ten months before her death, she was once again admitted to the cancer center. My mom was in immense pain and required a few days of pain management and a reevaluation of her medication and treatment. While at the center, she was given too much morphine. As a result of the overdose, her body went into shock and she had convulsions. Her breathing became shallow and she went into a coma for a short time. Some time after, my mother relayed the following story about her experience to my sister, Hanna. Khatie remembered that the doctor had raised her legs, presumably because she was in shock. She remembered seeing this from outside the body. She also remembered seeing my grandmother and my father. My grandmother had passed on about 20 years before this had happened and Hassan had died some six years before.

My mother also remembered seeing the spiritual leader to whom she had prayed as part of her religion. It is a common experience for people who have a near death experience or who pass on to see a guru or a spiritual leader whom they prayed to or were close to while on earth. For example, Christians may see Jesus. Hindus may see Krishna. These spiritual or religious leaders are there to make the dying person feel comfortable with the "after life" and also to act as a guide. The spiritual leader whom my mother saw told her that it was not yet time for her to come over to the spiritual realms. As she told my sister, Hanna, afterwards, the next thing she remembered was that she was back in her body again. Some time after the incident occurred, she wondered why she had to come back. Hanna explained to her that she probably hadn't finished her karma yet and still had some things to take care of in this physical existence.

When I heard about my mother's experience, I wondered whether it was an out of body or a near death experience. During an out of body experience, the soul usually wanders close to the body, visits the astral or spiritual plane or has some other "out of body" experience. During a near death experience, the soul might see a tunnel, a being of light, or relatives who have passed on to the spiritual realms. A near death experience is as close to the after death experience that a person can experience without actually dying. Also, for a near death experience to occur, the heart does not necessarily have to stop. I needed to clarify the experience, so I searched my bookshelf and studied books by Dr. Raymond Moody and Dr. Melvin Morse on these subjects. They described patients who were comatose or unconscious and had similar experiences to my mom. Based on this evidence, I assumed my mom had both, an out of body experience and a near death experience.

Out of Body Experiences are common

Out of body experiences occur when the soul leaves the body, but only temporarily. These experiences can also occur during sleep or in meditation. Many people during surgery have had out of body experiences during which time they view auras and other events in the operating room. The actress Jane Seymour recently mentioned to Arlene Bynon on her television show, *Bynon,* that she had an out of body experience but did not feel like going any further because of her responsibility to her children. Seymour also related to Bynon that Christopher Reeve had an out of body experience during his surgery. Many Buddhist monks have claimed that they have traveled to other planets during an out of body experience. Sometimes this experience is referred to as astral traveling.

Kevin Ryerson in his book, *Spirit Communication: The Soul's Path,* discusses an out of body experiment conducted by The American Society for Psychical Research. Two psychics, Ingo Swann and Harold Sherman, conducted the experiment in the early 1970s. This experiment yields strong evidence that consciousness transcends physical form. The two psychics were asked to leave their bodies or astral project and travel to Mercury and Jupiter to observe the atmosphere of the two planets. Researchers were hoping that NASA's probes that were due to orbit back within days would corroborate the information brought back by the psychics. The data from the probes showed that both Swann and Sherman accurately described certain previously unknown characteristics of the planet Mercury. Furthermore, the information was received "instantaneously" while NASA photos took about 6.5 minutes to get from point A to point B. They concluded that the speed of thought exceeds the speed of light. It also proved the capability and effectiveness of out of body experiences.

Reincarnation

If you don't believe in karma or reincarnation, don't worry. You probably will in your next life.

— Bruce Goldberg

Reincarnation is a belief system that is accepted by a large majority of the world's population. It makes logical sense, and it makes the individual responsible for his or her actions. I don't believe we are here for only one lifetime and then end up in either heaven or hell. This theory leaves too many unanswered questions such as the following: Where do new souls come from? Why are children so different from each other when they are born? Why are some people born with illnesses while others are not? Why are some born with handicaps? The theory of living only one lifetime raises more questions than answers. I believe the theory of reincarnation is more logical and is more realistic.

According to the great classic of Indian literature, the *Bhagavad-Gita*, "as a man casts off old clothes and puts on new ones, so the embodied self, casting off old bodies proceeds to other and new ones." Through the normal cycle of birth and death, we as souls have inhabited female as well as male bodies. And why don't we remember our lifetimes? Because it would not do us much good to learn that we had done a bad deed in a past life. A soul should not forget its purpose, to be at one with God. To go back to God might take many lifetimes. We in our souls carry memories or learnings of this lifetime and past lives. We are here to learn to be pure souls again. We can only climb the ladder to spiritual perfection through soul growth, one step at a time.

Although most people do not remember their previous reincarnations, I read a story about a girl in New Delhi, India who did so. Joe Fisher in his book, *The Case for Reincarnation*, talks about a girl named Reena Gupta. Reena was less than two years old when she began to recall a past life where she claimed her previous husband had killed her. As the years went on, she began to recall more previous life events. She also claimed that she had four children of her own. Reena began searching for her husband and children. Reena's bizarre behavior continued for five more years during which time her mother began making inquiries about a possible previous life. Her inquiries led her to the Singh family in another part of the city whose story seemed to match the one told by Reena. Intrigued by this situation, the Singh family visited Reena. When Reena saw the Singhs, she immediately recognized them and said with a big smile "They are my father and mother." The Guptas learned that the Singhs had a daughter named Gurdeep that had been killed by her husband, Surjeet, a few years ago. Surjeet was serving a prison sentence. The next day, Reena recognized Gurdeep's sister and immediately called her by her nickname. Reena also recognized a photograph of her as the late Gurdeep. When Reena was nine years old she met Surjeet. She was very fearful and reluctant to meet him. She said, "He will kill me again." However, when Reena met Gurdeep's four children, she was extremely joyful.

Joe Fisher also presents the story of another girl named Romy Crees from Des Moines, Iowa. As soon as she could talk, Romy said she was Joe Williams, husband of Sheila and father of three children. Romy said that she had died in a motorcycle accident and was now scared of them. She expressed a wish to go to Charles City where she once lived as Joe. Romy wanted to tell her "Mother Williams" that everything was fine. In 1981, Romy and her father visited Charles City, which is about 140 miles away from Des Moines. In Charles City, Romy met the mother and recognized a picture of Joe, Sheila and the children. Mrs. Williams confirmed the details of Joe's marriage to Sheila, the three children, names of other relatives and the 1975-motorcycle accident near Chicago in which Joe and Sheila were both killed. Other details mentioned by Romy also matched the details given by Mrs. Williams. Joe Williams had died two years before Romy was born. Mrs. Williams and the Crees were both devout Catholics and could not accept the concept of reincarnation. The mother, Bonnie Crees said, "I don't know how to explain it." She went on, "but I do know my daughter isn't lying."

Reincarnation is not mentioned only in Indian literature. It is mentioned in the Bible as well. According to some metaphysical philosophers, reincarnation was originally taught in the Bible but was removed in the year 553 A.D. by the Fifth Ecumenical Council in Constantinople. Students of Edgar Cayce believe there are still references in the Bible to reincarnation. One interesting one is where the Bible apparently refers to John the Baptist as the reincarnation of Elijah. To learn more about this, you might want to study Cayce. I recommend the book *Edgar Cayce: Reflections on the Path*, by Herbert B. Puryear Ph.D. In his other book, *The Edgar Cayce Primer,* Puryear mentions some interesting facts about reincarnation. He says that Cayce's readings indicate that "the reason reincarnation has not been retained in Christianity has been a desire to take shortcuts." Puryear mentions that by belonging to a certain organization or sect, people may feel that "they will in some special way find favor with God and thus be ushered directly into His presence upon their deaths." He mentions the teaching of "one life and after that eternal judgment is based in part on a kind of elitism." As a result, Puryear says that one group, which believes it has found "the true way," may feel superior over others. Furthermore, Puryear says the teaching – that there is one life – may lead to exploitation. He says that if a church or group has special access "to the way" that others do not have, they may wield a lot of control over individuals, groups or nations. Many organized religions claim that their way is the "only way." Although I respect their point-of-view, the theory of reincarnation levels the playing field. It assumes that everyone is equal in the eyes of God. Nobody is superior to anybody else. We are all on a common journey, and our final objective is to be one with God. Puryear says "it is only in terms of reincarnation that we can think of God as being truly fair, patient, loving, forgiving and all-merciful". He says that God wants all the lost souls to be back at one with him. Puryear explains that God "is the father of all souls; it is not His will that any soul should perish."

Is it a good idea to review your past lives? Although it is rare to remember a past life, a person can sometimes accomplish this by using hypnosis or past life regression techniques. I am aware of people who have found these techniques helpful in taking care of anxieties or other mental disorders. However, these techniques are not always successful. If you are interested in doing this, make sure that you deal with experienced professionals. First, I would recommend meditation, prayer and "knowing about yourself." In other words, inner analysis should be tried first. God is always there to help; all you have to do is ask and have patience.

The cycle of death and rebirth eventually ends

When does the cycle of birth and rebirth end for us? Although many books about Cayce have the answer to this question, a couple of books stood out for me. One was a book by Lynn Elwell Sparrow called *Reincarnation: Claiming Your Past, Creating Your Future*. The other book is *Reincarnation Unnecessary* by Violet M. Shelley. Shelley says that out of 1,200 people who came to Edgar Cayce for life readings, eighteen were told that when their lives ended on Earth, they might choose not to return to Earth. Let us not forget that a soul might have finished its karma or learning on Earth but it might have karma somewhere else. In Shelley's book, it has been referred to as "other realms for instruction." Sparrow in her book called it "other planes of consciousness." It is good to remember that these eighteen people had not reached soul perfection. They had just completed their karma on Earth. They had learnt their lessons here. As souls, we might still have karma in another planet or some other dimensions unknown to us at this time. Although our karma on Earth might be complete, we might use our free will and choose to come back for an unselfish mission? That is an option. We should not worry about questions such as where and when? Let's take life one day at a time. First, let's deal with our karma on Earth first.

We should not assume that just because we don't have to come back to Earth, we are ready to be at one with God. What attributes should we have to not return for another incarnation on Earth? The common attributes of the eighteen people that Shelley mentions are as follows: love of God and your fellow human being, service to others, unselfishness, tolerance, long suffering and learning from it, patience, forgiveness, kindness, and a purity of soul. The starting point of all of this is to know your own soul. That is where you will find God. Who decides how many incarnations we still have to go through? Do we know whether Mother Theresa will reincarnate again? How about Martin Luther King or Gandhi? As we go through our daily lives, we should not worry about these kinds of questions. We are not the judge and jury, are we? That is between your soul and God.

Sparrow includes a short story in her book. It is the story of a Buddhist master and his two disciples. The first disciple asks the master, "How many lives do I have to live before I reach enlightenment?" The master replies, "three more lives." The discouraged disciple goes back to his meditation. The second disciple asks the same question, "How many lives do I have to live before I reach enlightenment?" The master replies gravely, " I am afraid you still have one thousand lifetimes to go." "One thousand lifetimes!" exclaims the second disciple as he exultantly goes off dancing into the woods. And he instantly becomes enlightened. The message here is clear. Reincarnation is a part of your spiritual growth. You have led many past lives and probably will lead many more. Enjoy God's creation. Don't think of the voyage of life as a job or an event that you conduct grudgingly with disdain or apathy. As the English comedy group, Monty Python, says, "Always look on the bright side of life."

Responsibility for the future

…Believing as I do in the theory of rebirth, I live in the hope that if not in this birth, in some other birth I shall be able to hug all humanity in friendly embrace.

— Mohandas K. Gandhi

Each individual can have a positive influence on the future

In his book, *Soul Development*, Kevin Todeschi tells a story about Woodrow Wilson (1856-1924), the twenty-eighth president of the United States. He was president from 1913 to 1921, which included the tumultuous period of World War I. Todeschi mentions that although Wilson was not considered to be a very religious man, he worked extremely hard to achieve peace on Earth. After the war, he felt that the world needed a League of Nations. He was convinced that international cooperation on a global scale was key to establishing a peaceful world. His idea gained international support and was part of the Treaty of Versailles, which brought an end to World War I. In 1919, Wilson won the Nobel Peace Prize. The League was a predecessor to the United Nations. The important aspect of his work, I believe, was that Wilson thought that everyone on

Earth should work together to achieve peace, regardless of their religion, color, sex, or other aspects. Also, we don't have to be presidents to make a difference in the world. We can make a difference on our own corner of the world.

Princess Diana, who unfortunately left us too early, is an example of a person who made a difference. She was involved in many charitable causes. One of her personal crusades was to publicize the issue of land mines and how children had lost limbs and eyes and had become disfigured as a result. This had a major impact on me. Princess Diana made a major impact in this area, and everyone can make a positive impact in some area of his or her lives. Another example of making a positive contribution is the organization called "Doctors without Borders," which won the international Nobel Peace Prize in 1999. This organization is comprised of doctors who volunteer to give assistance to populations throughout the world "without discrimination and irrespective of race, religion, creed or political affiliation." It is a very worthwhile, admirable and selfless cause.

Recently, I read an article about the richest man in the world, Bill Gates. He and his wife Melinda have donated $995 million US to international health, education and technology programs. I found it very heartwarming to see some of this well-earned money going to worthwhile causes. There are many people, rich and poor, who give to charities to help the poor and the needy. That is a commendable act. They are great mentors for everyone.

Now is the time to heed signs that our planet is in trouble

A report called *Climate Change 2001: Impacts, Adaptation and Vulnerability*, was released by the United Nations in Geneva, Switzerland. The report did an extensive investigation into the effects of global warming on different countries and regions of the world. The report, summarizing more than 1,000 pages of research conducted by some 700 scientists throughout the world, brought forward some disturbing predictions and concerns. The scientists placed the blame for global warming on the use of carbon-based fossil fuels, industrial pollution and the destruction of forests among other factors. They predicted that global devastation might occur because of the accelerated rate of environmental change caused by the accumulation of carbon dioxide and other greenhouse gases. The scientists revealed that global warming is likely to lead to an increase in extreme weather conditions and could result in a greater frequency of floods, cyclones and droughts. The food and water supply of the planet will be affected, sea levels will rise causing floods, diseases will increase and coral reefs will be damaged.

Terrible environmental consequences such as those outlined by these scientists are exactly what psychics such as Nostradamus have predicted will occur in the future. Some people who have experienced near death experiences have also brought back similar catastrophic information. Throughout the ages, many such warnings have been given. Are we, as inhabitants who share this common planet called Earth, going to do something about this? We have the free will to either pressure governments to be more active in dealing with this largely man made mess or to say nothing and suffer the environmental consequences. Each of us can make a difference.

Spirit Guides and Angels

I am well aware that many will say that no one can possibly speak with spirits and angels as long as he lives in the body...But by all this I am not deterred, for I have seen, I have heard, I have felt.

— Emanuel Swedenborg

Guides help people on their spiritual journeys

Spirit guides are always there to assist people in their spiritual path. Some children, most of them before the age of two to four, see invisible people or imaginary friends. Parents might wonder, "Who are these children talking to?" They could be interacting and playing with their spirit guides and angels. Children are able to do this because they are fresh, newly born souls from the spiritual world. They still have close spiritual connections to that world. As the children get older and become more entrenched in the physical world, they can become more distant from the spiritual world. Then these spirit guides no longer appear to the children in their waking state but may appear in their sleeping or dreaming states. When adults become psychically attuned to the spiritual world through activities such as meditation, spirit guides can once again appear to help or guide them. Sometimes, spirit guides appear in people's dreams although they might not remember them when they awake. And when people pass over to the spiritual world, they see their spirit guides again.

As you go through life's many changes and phases, different guides will appear to assist you. Guides who are experienced in the particular phase that you are going through will come forward at that time. When people are having difficulties in their lives, spirit guides might appear more frequently during their dreaming or meditative states. This is why some people find that their stress decreases after taking a short nap or getting a good night's sleep. It is probably a combination of rest, assistance from spirit guides, and analysis and problem solving by their own souls. People can also see spirit guides when they have an out of body or a near death experience. Should you try to establish closer contact with their guide? Many people make the extra effort to get in touch with their spirit guides through spiritual or meditative exercises. I believe it is better to not force the issue. If the relationship comes, it will come naturally.

Who are these spirit guides? They might be people from past lives. In his book, *Spirit Communication: The Soul's Path*, Kevin Ryerson says that spirit guides come to us so that we "may express to them and may learn from their philosophy, insight, and the context of their cultural understanding. For they desire to project understanding of an empathic nature." He says, "As you progress, so in turn do the spirit guides and teachers about your progress. Above all else, you promote one another's well being." Ryerson says that spirit guides are usually "members of your soul group" but in a discarnate or spirit state. By soul group, I think he means that we have known each other from past lives. Ryerson also differentiates between spirit guides and teachers. He says that spirit guides deal with emotions and teachers deal with ethics. Ryerson says that if "you are emotionally upset, a guide takes priority. If you are going through a career decision, a teacher takes priority." Ryerson says that spirit guides and teachers do not enter your body but merely "overshadow" you. In terms of control and final decisions making, Ryerson stresses, "ultimately, your best source of guidance is your own inner divine." He says "the final decisions all lie with the individual in the affairs of the spirit." Guides might advise us but people have free will and that should always dictate their final decisions. Trance channelers, mediums and some psychics can set aside their consciousness and allow spirit guides to speak through them. Most of these spirit guides provide important spiritual information. For example, Kevin Ryerson, allowed entities such as John and Tom MacPherson to speak through him. I believe it is important to focus on the information that is being conveyed – the message itself – rather than the messenger. With regards to prayer, Ryerson and other channelers always stress over and over that we should not pray to a guide but only to God. I also believe that people should never pray to a guide. I pray and meditate only to God and have found help and assistance in this manner. Life flows more smoothly when a person is more spiritually attuned because the creative forces or God always look after them. I believe that God will never desert His children.

Angels are also there to help people on their spiritual paths

Good night, sweet prince. And flights of Angels sing thee to thy rest.

— Hamlet

Sayings such as "I feel guided," or "I have an angel looking after me" or "I have an angel on my shoulder" are common in the world today – and perhaps this is because they are true! Every person on this Earth has an angel looking after him or her. Some people mistake angels for spirit guides and vice versa. The word "angel" comes from the Greek word for messenger. Angels are more spiritually enlightened than spirit guides. In his book, *Spirit Communication: The Soul's Path*, Kevin Ryerson says, "Angels are beings who have never incarnated and still dwell in states of perfection." In the wonderful book, "*Do you have a Guardian Angel?*" author John Ronner talks about Emanuel Swedenborg. Swedenborg was one of the top scientists in the 1700s. In his fifties, Swedenborg went into trances for days at a time during which he claimed to visit the spirit world. Swedenborg said that maturing human souls gradually become angels in the after life. I feel that both Ryerson and Swedenborg are both correct. Some angels have never incarnated on earth and some enlightened souls do become angels. Ronner also says that angels are mentioned 300 times in the Bible and fifteen times by Jesus himself. He also mentions that the philosopher Socrates relied on a guardian angel and Joan of Arc who freed France from the English claimed she saw angels several times a week. In his book *The Meaning of the Glorious Koran*, Mohammed Marmaduke Pickthall talks about Prophet Mohammad's vision at Mount Hira. According to Pickthall, angel Gabriel appeared to the Prophet and told him "thou art Allah's messenger."

There are many books available on angels. Angels are beings of light. When people see them, they sometimes see them with wings on their backs. Why is this so? Well, throughout history, Christian artists and famous painters such as Rembrandt, Botticelli, Raphael and Chagall have painted angels with wings to portray them as being in flight. In reality, I don't think angels have wings. They are luminous souls and they do not need wings to move through space and time. Perhaps angels sometimes appear with wings because they assume people are more comfortable with this concept. I think children and adults have associated angels with wings based on their upbringing and religious art. The early books of the Old Testament make no mention of angels with wings. When Edgar Cayce was young, an angel with wings visited him. The angel asked him what he wanted to do with his life. He said that he wanted to help people, especially sick children. That is what he did with his more than 14,000 spiritual readings.

Intuition can alert a person to a spiritual presence

My intuition has proven useful in advising me of a spiritual presence. Late one night, I was heavily into writing this book. I was into the "writer's groove" where information was flowing as if someone had opened up a water tap. All of a sudden, I felt a very strong presence behind me. It was so strong that I jerked and turned back in my revolving chair. I think I felt the hair at the back of my head bristle. As I turned around, I looked and I could not see anything. Yet I could feel a presence. As I turned back to face my computer monitor, the first picture that came to my mind was that of a monk wearing a hood. But I could not see a face. I said a little prayer to God and after a few seconds, I felt the presence leave, move upwards and disappear.

I went to bed wondering who this entity was. The entity or soul did not seem threatening in any way. I had a feeling that the entity was there to observe me. I hoped it liked my writing. Perhaps it was helping me in some way? Perhaps it had come to visit my mom who was resting in the next room? From my readings, I think it could have been one of three entities. It could have been a spirit guide, an angel or an earthbound entity. When I said my prayer, I felt it go away so I knew that this entity was respectful. I took this visit as a positive sign. I felt I was getting encouragement from the spiritual realms to keep writing.

I have felt energies around me many times while writing this book. But I have never experienced such a strong presence as that one. I am very grateful that God is always there to help me and protect me. It's very hard for me to put into words how I feel about God's love. All I can say is that once I experienced it, nothing on Earth has compared to it. The feeling I get from connecting with God is incredibly peaceful, loving and energizing. I hope that my path leads me where I can experience more of God's beauty and love whether in this dimension or some other. I look forward to the journey and hope my spirit guides help me along the way.

Suicide

...it is said many times that you can easily cheat others but you can never fool yourself or the infinite light — you have to face up to yourself.

— George Anderson

Suicide is not a solution to problems but only a postponement

In the United States, suicide is the ninth leading cause of death as over 32,000 people commit suicide each year. It is estimated that a suicide is committed every minute. Suicide is the second leading cause of death among college students in the States. Thankfully, in 1999 the Surgeon General, who is the top public health official in the United States, declared suicide a serious health threat for the first time. Why did it take so long? Suicide occurs in every culture and nation in the world from Australia to China, from Malaysia to England. Everyday in the newspapers, on television or on the Internet, I see and read about common everyday people as well as famous people committing suicide. How about twenty-seven year old Kurt Cobain of the musical group Nirvana who killed himself with a gun? Such potential and talent gone in an instant! I recently read about an eighty-year-old actor named Richard Farnsworth, who committed suicide at 80 years of age.

He was the oldest leading actor ever to receive an Oscar nomination.

Let us go deeper into the spiritual ramifications of this event called suicide. Suicide is only a postponement and never a release from a person's current difficulties. A person who commits suicide will come back in the next life with the same problems that he or she had in this life, and more! More problems because they caused grief to other people whom they left behind and they take that with them as an imprint in their souls. A mother's grief, a wife's sorrows, a child left fatherless or motherless, and incomplete responsibilities.

Anyone who is considering committing suicide might benefit from watching the 1946 film classic, *A Wonderful Life*, starring James Stewart as George Bailey. Bailey is about to jump off a bridge when an angel appears and shows him the affect he has had upon family and friends by being on Earth. When Bailey sees how he has contributed to the lives of the people around him, he decides not to jump. *A Wonderful Life* is a very touching story. It illustrates the concept that everyone has a purpose for being here. And everything is connected. If you are experiencing difficulties in life, try to get help from others rather than going through it alone.

A soul usually regrets committing suicide

If people succeed in killing themselves, what do they face? After my suicide crisis I wondered about this question. I read *A Soul's Journey* by Peter Richelieu. This is a true story. Richelieu was in a state of despair because of his brother's death. Acharya, an Indian mystic, visited him. Using astral projection, Acharya took Richelieu out of the physical world and onto the astral planes. In the process, he was exposed to spiritual teachings on topics such as death and karma. According to what Richelieu wrote in *A Soul's Journey*, this is what happens to someone who commits suicide: Usually a soul who leaves the body after committing suicide is remorseful. After the soul arrives in the astral world, it would do anything to undo its actions. Unfortunately, these actions cannot be undone. The soul knows that it will have to wait until the next life where it will have to face the same difficulties again. At that time, it will have the opportunity to make another choice.

After leaving the body, a soul might realize that what it has done is wrong, and might not be ready to go to the astral world. This soul is considered to be "earthbound." Other souls who have passed away in the "normal way" do get help from astral helpers or spirit guides. Depending on the circumstances, a soul who has committed suicide might not get sympathetic help from its guides right away because of its actions. In this case, Richelieu says that a soul might feel alone, as it does not belong in the physical world or the spiritual world. The soul is stuck in this "no man's land." As a result, the soul might wander about the places where it took its life. Because of its loneliness and potential bitterness toward humankind, it might try to convince other souls to join it. This rarely happens, but if it succeeds, it will take on more karma and more things to learn in the next life. However, after a period of time, the soul might become more cooperative and then it will receive a helping hand from an astral helper or guide. After entering the astral planes, the soul has a review and is shown the impact its suicide will have on the people it left behind. The soul learns that it will inherit the pain of those it hurt as well. Richelieu reaffirms the fact that a suicide is never a release but a postponement of your current difficulties. According to Richelieu (and I agree with him) suicide is not really worth it, is it?

Mediums such as George Anderson and James Van Praagh communicate with souls who have passed on. In their respective books, *Lessons from the Light* and *Talking to Heaven* they received the following information: They have said that souls who have committed suicide do not recommend it as an easy way out of earthly struggles and problems. These souls have mentioned that in the astral world, they have a long road of forgiveness, understanding and healing to go through. They mention that to attain soul development, it is better to deal with problems while on earth no matter how tough and insurmountable they may appear to be. Anderson mentions that time on earth in finite while time in the spiritual realms is infinite. As a result, it takes much less time to learn on earth than in the spiritual realms. Earth is our learning ground. There are no shortcuts to spiritual development. Families who are left on earth may be left with a sense of guilt because of a suicide of a close family member. Souls who have passed on usually ask for forgiveness and prayers from people they have left behind on earth. These souls receive counseling, help and compassion from family members, friends and even pets that have passed on. The teachings of many churches proclaim that souls who commit suicide end up in hell. Information received from mediums claim that this is not the case. The souls who have passed on are fine and are not being tortured by the devil. I believe that God is not a vengeful or merciless God. He is a loving and caring Father who has given us free will and wants us to come back to him when we are ready.

People who attempt suicide become stronger afterwards

When written in Chinese, the word crisis is composed of two characters. One represents danger and the other represents opportunity.
— John F. Kennedy

Unfortunately, in many societies throughout the world, there is still a stigma attached to committing suicide. Some social groups might also ridicule the families of people who attempt to commit suicide. This is unfortunate. It means that their society is not forgiving, which is a bad spiritual trait. Instead, showing compassion, respect, kindness, generosity and unconditional love is very important in these matters. People who are able to come out of their depressions often become much stronger psychologically and emotionally. They become better souls and they often vow never to sink so low again. And they usually don't. More and more, both ordinary and famous people are coming out and telling how they have turned something negative into something positive. This is commendable because these people can become mentors to depressed teenagers and adults who might be thinking of committing this dreadful act.

Five years ago, when he was 20 years old, a friend of mine, Brian, tried to commit suicide using a gun. His aim was off. Instead of killing himself, Brian became blind in both eyes. His family was devastated. He was treated for depression, which is a common illness in these situations. However, Brian mentioned to me that he had learnt his lesson and believed that his actions were wrong. He was positive about his future, wanted to help people in some way and had moved into his own apartment. Recently I saw him at a record store where he was purchasing some Garth Brooks CDs. Sometimes the blind see more than those who are sighted. Brian also has faith in God, which I believe is a very positive sign.

One of my favorite vocalists, Billy Joel, was once in such a depressive state that he considered suicide. He was broke, sleeping in Laundromats and his girlfriend had left him. Luckily, Joel checked himself into a hospital. That episode was one of the best things that happened to him because it turned around his life. After his suicide crisis, Joel went on to become a great songwriter and musician. He also married a famous model, Christie Brinkley, and together they had a beautiful daughter, Alexa Ray. Would all this success have happened if he had killed himself?

Once I attended a lecture in Calgary, Canada by Anthony Robbins. He is the author of the book *Awaken the Giant Within*. The book gives knowledge on increasing Self-awareness and taking control of your mental, emotional, physical and financial destiny. He signed the book for me and wrote, "Live with passion." I agree with him wholeheartedly, live with plenty of passion! Set a goal for your life and try to attain it. First, you have to make the effort. It might be hard work but the rewards are plentiful. Life is short, so live it! Don't be a follower; be a leader and take action. Let go of your pride and ego and ask for help if you require it.

UFOs

In my youth I regarded the universe as an open book, printed in the language of physical equations, whereas now it appears to me as a text written in invisible ink, of which in our rare moments of grace we are able to decipher a small fragment.

— Arthur Koestler

As part of my spiritual investigations, I attended a conference in Banff, Canada a few years ago. I never told my friends or family about it until recently because of a fear of ridicule. The conference was about UFOs. There were people at the conference that claimed to have been abducted by extraterrestrials. When they spoke of their experiences, the abductees were under hypnosis. Some of the abductors talked about their bodies being lifted out of their beds and in a sense being kidnapped. Some of them seemed to be in real pain and were crying under hypnosis. Consciously, they did not remember the abduction. When I say "consciously," I am referring to our five senses. Perhaps the brain, which is physical, could have been programmed by the extraterrestrials to forget the memory. Hypnosis taps into our subconscious thoughts. The soul remembers everything. Many people have remembered past lives under hypnosis.

The UFO conference was fascinating, strange, and disturbing all at the same time. After the conference, I drove back home alone that night looking up at the sky as well as looking behind myself in the back seat. I saw a falling star in the sky but no UFO. I don't think I will ever forget that experience. I have always wondered whether the abductees were hired actors. I don't think they were. Abductions don't seem to be too much fun. If I met an extraterrestrial, I would have many questions about the meaning of life, spirituality, and UFOs. I would like to spend lots of time with that being so I would hope that it would not be in a hurry to take the next ship back to the Pleiades.

However, I believe that extraterrestrials do visit us. Many people have taken pictures of their spacecrafts. Extraterrestrials have been visiting Earth for millions of years. I will not spend too much time giving examples of famous encounters such as the landing at Roswell, New Mexico, or other events. There are many books and documentaries on this topic. I recommend books such as *Out On A Limb* by Shirley MacLaine, as well as *Intruders* by Budd Hopkins and *Encounters* by Dr. Edith Fiore. Even the famous psychoanalyst, Carl G. Jung investigated this phenomenon and wrote a book in 1958 called *Flying Saucers: A Modern Myth Of Things Seen In The Sky*. So where do these extraterrestrials come from? According to some theories, when God created souls billions of years ago, some of these souls inhabited Earth. Other souls went to distant planets, galaxies, and solar systems in our universe. These extraterrestrials are our soul brothers and sisters. Initially I had a hard time believing this. But it is a theory that is often discussed in metaphysical literature. Moreover, extraterrestrials are spiritual beings and so they also believe in God. Similar to people, extraterrestrials are on their own learning paths and have to follow the laws of karma and reincarnation as well.

Extraterrestrials are concerned about our use of technology and weapons of destruction

Extraterrestrials are technologically and probably spiritually more advanced than people are. They watch over us and usually observe around key technical areas such as military installations. So why are they here? To give a simple analogy, just as people observe other animals to learn about their lifestyles, extraterrestrials are paying attention to people in the same way. Among other things, they are concerned about Earth's environment and people's misuse of technology and nuclear and biological weapons — basically any weapons of destruction. There appear to be more sightings of UFOs during times of major crisis on Earth. This is because the extraterrestrials are concerned about the future of humankind and are keeping an eye on Earth. Contrary to what is sometimes depicted in Hollywood movies, extraterrestrials are not here to invade Earth. With their vastly superior technology they could destroy Earth in an instant but they will not do that.

I know it seems far-fetched, but is it possible that people — as spiritual beings — might have encountered these extraterrestrial souls in some other past life? In MacLaine's book, *Out on a Limb*, David (Shirley's guide) mentions that the mountain people of the Andes in Peru witness UFOs on a regular basis and are not disturbed by them. MacLaine says that they are so relaxed about it that they have a sign at the highest railway point in the world, which says, "Flying Saucers do exist. UFO contact point." I don't believe extraterrestrials mean to harm people. Their objective is not to interfere in the "natural progression" of the planet. These extraterrestrials know that human beings on Earth have their own karma to deal with. Plus, many people are not ready to interact with them; however, someday that might change. I am aware of psychics who claim to be in contact with extraterrestrials. Most of the messages that they convey are about spiritual growth and peace.

Claims that important sites such as the Pyramid of Giza in Egypt, Machu Picchu in Peru, Stonehenge in England, and Inca and Mayan landmarks among others were built with the assistance of extraterrestrials could be true. The Inca and Mayan calendars are accurate even though they were produced thousands of years ago. Astronomical data, which could only be available to a highly evolved species, appears to be responsible for this data. In religious stories such as the *Mahabharata*, there is talk of flying machines and heavenly lights coming down from the sky. The first chapter of the Book of Ezekiel also talks about creatures on "wheels" coming from the sky. The ancients talked about gods coming down from the sky. Could they be talking about UFOs? I recently saw a documentary about the building of the pyramids. The scientists were trying to discover how the Egyptians managed to cut those huge rocks in such a precise pattern. They also wanted to ascertain how the Egyptians lifted the huge blocks of which the pyramids were made. The scientists discussed various interesting theories including help from extraterrestrials.

The study of UFOs is an interesting one. It is getting more credibility in the new millennium as more people witness and record UFO sightings. Jimmy Carter, the former president of the United States, once saw a UFO. Until then he was a skeptical man. Area 51 in the Nevada desert is well known among UFO investigators. I believe that information gathered from this site was recently moved to another secret location, but air space is still restricted above Area 51. A few years ago a scientist who apparently worked at Area 51 went to the media because his life was threatened. He claimed that this site is the place where scientists are investigating and experimenting with spacecraft and possibly the bodies of extraterrestrials. Could the spacecraft and extraterrestrial bodies be the ones from the crash that occurred near Roswell, New Mexico? Apparently, the objective of scientists on Earth is to study and apply the advanced UFO technology for military and security purposes. I hope it helps human kind and does not destroy it. I guess this is where the concept of free will comes into affect. What is the scientists' motive in using this technology? I believe that people need to remember that spirituality is important and that the connection to God is critical.

Epilogue

One of the 20th century's greatest leaders, Mohandas Gandhi once said, "I am a Muslim, and a Hindu, and a Christian, and a Jew - and so are all of you." His message was simple yet extremely effective. His message was that all of us are part of the same spiritual family. I believe religions have an important place in our spiritual lives. However, religions and their dogmas and doctrines may create a feeling of superiority over others and as a result may separate us as soul brothers and sisters. We may forget that we are the same inside, in our souls and that we have the same spiritual objectives, desires and feelings. I hope we realize that although we may be separated by denominations, doctrines and beliefs we come from the one source, God.

I believe that we cannot leave the responsibility for the most important thing in our lives – that of our soul and our spiritual life — to external institutions. We need to be leaders and not followers. If you have questions about spirituality and meaning of life issues, it is your responsibility to attain that knowledge. With this book, I hope I can do my small part to help you in your spiritual search.

If someone asked me, "What are two important things required in life?" I would say Have faith and Attain knowledge. I have found immense strength from my faith in God. That is very important to me. Knowledge has provided me with an understanding of the meaning of life. As a result of these two things, I have become a much happier individual.

To my fellow spiritual traveler, I hope that your journey brings you spiritual and personal growth, happiness, love, and inner peace.

Bibliography

Ailments, handicaps, and the question — "Why me?"
See Karma & Reincarnation

Akashic Records

MacLaine, Shirley. *Out on a Limb*. New York: Bantam Books, 1984. (See Chapters 11, 14, and 23 for references to the "Out On a Limb" quote.)

Todeschi, Kevin J. *Edgar Cayce on the Akashic Records*. Virginia Beach: A.R.E. Press, 1998. (Highly recommended book, which provides extensive detail and case histories of the Akashic Records.)

Animal Souls

Anderson, George and Andrew Barone. *Lessons from the Light*. New York: G.P. Putnam's Sons, 1999. (See Chapter 10 for a discussion on animals in the spiritual world.)

Cerminara, Gina. *Many Lives, Many Loves*. New York: Signet Books, 1974. (Look at chapter 7 for an interesting discussion on reincarnation and animals.)

Manes, Christopher. *Other Creations: Rediscovering the Spirituality of Animals*. New York: Doubleday, 1997. (Great book on animals and their spiritual influence on humankind.)

McGraw, Carol. *Do Pets Have Souls? Religious Teachings Vary*. Seattle: Seattle Times, January 23, 1999.

Richelieu, Peter. *A Soul's Journey*. London: The Aquarian Press, 1989. (See Chapter 9, pages 133 to 135 for a discussion about group souls.)

Stein, Barbara. *Animal Souls, Reincarnation, and the Return of Snoopy—the Lunchmeat Lambada King*. (Interview with Linda Madrid). Tempe: Natural Paws News, Volume II, Fall 1996.

Auras

Agee, Doris. *Edgar Cayce on ESP*. New York: Warner Books, 1988. (See Chapter 7 on auras from a Cayce perspective.)

Bro, Harmon H. *Edgar Cayce: On Religion and Psychic Experience*. New York: Warner Books, 1988. (See Chapter 5 on auras).

Burns, Litany. *Develop Your Psychic Abilities*. New York: Pocket Books, 1987. (See Chapter 6 on auras.)

Fuller, Elizabeth. *Everyone is Psychic*. New York: Crown Publishers, Inc., 1989. (See chapter 8 for information on auras.)

Sanders Jr., Pete A. *You are Psychic*. New York: Fawcett Columbine Books, 1990. (See Chapter 6 on sensing an aura.)

Ward, Tara. *Discover Your Psychic Powers*. London: Arcturus Publishing Limited, 2000. (See chapter 4 for a description and discussion of an aura.)

Birth

Chadwick, Gloria. *Discovering Your Past Lives*. Chicago: Contemporary Books, 1988. (Look at chapter 13 for a discussion on what happens before birth.)

Fisher, Joe. *The Case for Reincarnation*. Toronto: Collins Publishers, 1984. (See chapter 4 on child prodigies.)

McGarey, William and Gladys McGarey. *Edgar Cayce's Readings on Home and Marriage*. New York: Bantam Books, 1987.(Look at Chapter 8, page 118 on the souls' entry into the body. Also see chapter 11 for a good discussion on birth and some possible reasons for a miscarriage.)

McGarey, William. *In Search of Healing*. New York: Perigee Books, 1996. (See chapter 13 for an interesting discussion on the soul's journey.)

Whitton, Joel L. and Joe Fisher. *Life Between Life*. New York: Warner Books, 1986. (See chapter 4 for an interesting discussion on choices made before birth.)

Chakras

Bethards, Betty. *Techniques for Health and Wholeness*. Novato: Inner Light Foundation, 1985. (See chapter 2 for a good description of the chakras.)

Leadbeater, C.W. *The Chakras*. Wheaton: Quest Books, 1990.

MacLaine, Shirley. *Going Within*. New York: Bantam Books, 1991. (See Chapter 8 on techniques to meditate on the chakras.)

McGarey, William. *In Search of Healing*. New York: Perigee Books, 1996. (See chapter 8 for an interesting discussion on the seven spiritual centers.)

Ryerson, Kevin and Stephanie Harolde. *Spirit Communication: The Soul's Path*. New York: Bantam Books, 1991. (See Part 3, Chapter 3, pages 229 to 238 for a good discussion about the chakras.)

Selby, John. *Kundalini Awakening*. New York: Bantam Books, 1992. (Look at part 2 on awakening of the energy centers.)

Sieczka, Helmut G. *Chakra Breathing*. Mendocino: LifeRhythm, 1994.

Wallace, Amy and Bill Henkin. *The Psychic Healing Book*. Oakland: Wingbow Press, 1992. (See Chapter 1, pages 25 to 31 on the chakras.)

Ward, Tara. *Discover Your Psychic Powers*. London: Arcturus Publishing Limited, 2000. (See chapter 5 for a description of the chakras and techniques on chakra awareness.)

Death

Anderson, George and Andrew Barone. *Lessons from the Light*. New York: G.P. Putnam's Sons, 1999.(Great book containing information from souls who have passed on.)

Belhayes, Iris. *Spirit Guides*. San Diego: ACS Publications, 1993. (Look at chapter 7 on the death experience.)

Bethards, Betty. *Be Your Own Guru*. Petaluma: Inner Light Foundation, 1991. (See chapter 3 for an excellent discussion on death and the astral planes.)

Fairchilde, Lily. *Song of the Phoenix*. New York: St. Martin's Press, 1997. (Excellent stories about death and the afterlife from people who have passed on.) Georgian, Linda. *Communicating with the Dead*. New York: Fireside Books, 1995.

Guggenheim, Bill and Judy Guggenheim. *Hello From Heaven!* New York: Bantam Books, 1997. (Great book on After-Death Communications.)

Hilarion. Threshold: *A Letter for Michelle*. Toronto: Marcus Books, 1985. (Look at chapter 11 on death and the astral realms.)

Martin, Joel and Patricia Romanowski. *We Don't Die: George Anderson's Conversations with the Other Side*. New York: Berkley Books, 1989.

Matthews, Dale with Connie Clark. *The Faith Factor*. New York: Viking Books, 1998. (See chapter 7 about how some Christians deal with upcoming death.)

Ramtha. *Ramtha* (Edited by Steven Lee Weinberg.) Eastbound: Sovereignty Inc., 1986. (See chapter 6 and 7 for an interesting discussion on life and death.)

Ryerson, Kevin and Stephanie Harolde. *Spirit Communication: The Soul's Path*. New York: Bantam Books, 1991. (Excellent book. See Part 3, Chapter 3, pages 238 to 247 about the process of death and the afterlife.)

Sechrist, Elsie R. *Death Does Not Part Us*. New York: St. Martin's Paperbacks, 1999. (See esp. Chapter 2, titled "Death and Re-birth.")

Scott, Claire. *Butterfly Blessings*. Calgary: Butterfly Blessings Publishers, 1999. (A "little" book on the process of dying by a palliative care nurse.

Sullivan, Eileen. *Arthur Ford Speaks From Beyond*. Greenwich: Fawcett Crest Books, 1976.

Van Praagh, James. *Talking To Heaven: A Medium's Message of Life After Death*. New York: Dutton Books, 1997.

___. *Reaching To Heaven: A Spiritual Journey Through Life and Death*. New York: Dutton Books, 1999. (Excellent book: See chapter 4 on death and chapter 5 on the spiritual realms.)

Yogananda, Paramahansa. *Where there is Light*. Los Angeles: Self-Realization Fellowship, 1989. (Great book. See Chapter 12 on understanding death.)

Dreams

Agee, Doris. *Edgar Cayce on ESP*. New York: Warner Books, 1988. (See Chapter 14. A good small chapter on dreams.)

Ball, Pamela. *10,000 Dreams Interpreted*. Great Britain: Prospero Books, 2001. (An A to Z on interpreting symbols in dreams.)

Bethards, Betty. *The Dream Book: Symbols for Self-Understanding*. Petaluma: Inner Light Foundation, 1994. (Great book on dreams and their symbols.)

Bro, Harmon H. *Edgar Cayce on Dreams*. New York: Warner Books, 1988.

Chadwick, Gloria. *Discovering Your Past Lives*. Chicago: Contemporary Books, 1988. (Look at chapter 10 for a discussion on past lives and dreams.)

Fuller, Elizabeth. *Everyone is Psychic*. New York: Crown Publishers, Inc., 1989. (See chapter 6 for a good discussion on dreams.)

Puryear, Herbert B. *The Edgar Cayce Primer*. New York: Bantam Books, 1982. (See chapter 16, pages 131 to 140 for a good discussion on dreams.)

Reed, Henry. *Awakening Your Psychic Powers*. New York: St. Martin's Paperbacks, 1996. (Look at chapter 5 for a discussion on dreams as a psychic doorway.)

Sechrist, Elsie. *Dreams: Your Magic Mirror*. New York: Warner Paperback Library, 1974.

Drugs and other short-term "highs"

Belhayes, Iris. *Spirit Guides*. San Diego: ACS Publications, 1993. (Look at chapter 8, page 133 on the impact of drugs on the body and soul.)

LeShan, Lawrence. *How to Meditate*. New York: Bantam Books, 1988. (See Chapter 3, pages 24 to 25 on differences between drugs and meditation.)

Matthews, Dale with Connie Clark. *The Faith Factor*. New York: Viking Books, 1998. (See chapter 5 on regaining freedom from addictions, from a Christian and spiritual perspective.)

Zukav, Gary. *The Seat of the Soul*. New York: Fireside Books, 1990. (See Chapter 10, pages 148 to 160 for a discussion on addictions.)

Free will and pre-destiny

Langley, Noel. *Edgar Cayce on Reincarnation*. New York: Warner Books, 1988. (See chapter 3, pages 47 to 48 for a discussion of free will and destiny.)

McGarey, William. *In Search of Healing*. New York: Perigee Books, 1996. (See chapter 7 for an interesting discussion on the power of choice.)

Montgomery, Ruth. *The World Before*. New York: Fawcett Crest Books, 1990. (Look at chapter 14 on prognostications.)

Puryear, Herbert B. *The Edgar Cayce Primer*. New York: Bantam Books, 1982. (See chapters 12 on our gift of free will.)

Ryerson, Kevin and Stephanie Harolde. *Spirit Communication: The Soul's Path*. New York: Bantam Books, 1991. (See Part 2, Chapter 1, pages 64-65 for a discussion of free will and pre-destiny.)

Sparrow, Lynn Elwell. *Reincarnation: Claiming Your Past, Creating Your Future*. New York: St. Martin's Paperbacks, 1995. (See Chapter 7 for a discussion on free will.)

Todeschi, Kevin J. *Edgar Cayce on the Akashic Records*. Virginia Beach: A.R.E. Press, 1998. (Excellent read. See Preface and all sections on past, present and the future.)

___. *Soul Development*. Virginia Beach: A.R.E. Press, 2000. (See Chapter 6 for a discussion on the nature of the human will.)

The History of Souls

Church, W.H. *Edgar Cayce's Story of the Soul*. Virginia Beach: A.R.E. Press, 1991. (A 252-page book on details of our soul history — highly recommended.)

MacLaine, Shirley. *The Camino*. New York: Pocket Books, 2000. (See Chapter 15 for a discussion on our soul history.)

Montgomery, Ruth. *The World Before*. New York: Fawcett Crest Books, 1990. (Good book on our soul history.)

Robinson, Lytle. *Edgar Cayce's Story of the Origin and Destiny of Man*. New York: Berkley Books, 1976.

Ryerson, Kevin and Stephanie Harolde. *Spirit Communication: The Soul's Path*. New York: Bantam Books, 1991. (See Part 2, Chapter 3, pages 75 to 78 for a brief history of our soul.)

Sparrow, Lynn Elwell. *Reincarnation: Claiming Your Past, Creating Your Future*. New York: St. Martin's Paperbacks, 1995. (See chapter 3 for a good discussion of our soul history.)

Karma

Bethards, Betty. *Be Your Own Guru*. Petaluma: Inner Light Foundation, 1991. (See chapter 2 on karma and reincarnation.)

Cerminara, Gina. *The World Within*. Virginia Beach: A.R.E. Press, 1988. (Look at Chapter 10 for karmic aspects of sex. Look at Chapter 14 for information on race and karma.)

McGarey, William and Gladys McGarey. *Edgar Cayce's Readings on Home and Marriage*. New York: Bantam Books, 1987. (Look at Chapter 2 for a good discussion on karma.)

Langley, Noel. *Edgar Cayce on Reincarnation*. New York: Warner Books, 1988. (See chapters 4, 5, and 6 on Karma. See chapter 16 on group karma. See chapter 15 on the Law of Grace.)

Montgomery, Ruth. *Here and Hereafter*. New York: Fawcett Crest Books, 1991. (See chapter 9 for an interesting discussion on group karma.)

Puryear, Herbert B. *The Edgar Cayce Primer.* New York: Bantam Books, 1982. (See chapter 11 for a discussion on karma and grace.)

Ryerson, Kevin and Stephanie Harolde. *Spirit Communication: The Soul's Path.* New York: Bantam Books, 1991. (See Part 2, Chapter 1, pages 65 to 68 on the concept of karma. Also see part 3, chapter 1, pages 111 to 115 on the law of grace.)

Sharma, I.C. *Cayce, Karma & Reincarnation.* Wheaton: Quest books, 1975. (See Chapter 7, pages 90 to 107 for a discussion on the doctrine of karma.)

Sparrow, Lynn Elwell. *Reincarnation: Claiming Your Past, Creating Your Future.* New York: St. Martin's Paperbacks, 1995. (See Parts 2 and 3 for a detailed discussion on karma.)

Woodward, Mary Ann. *Edgar Cayce's Story of Karma.* New York: Berkley Books, 1972. (Great book. Look at chapter 3 for physical karma and chapter 5 for family relationships.)

Zukav, Gary. *The Seat of the Soul.* New York: Fireside Books, 1990. (See Chapter 2, Pages 33 to 46 for a discussion of karma.)

Marriage, sex and soul mates

Hilarion. *Threshold: A Letter for Michelle.* Toronto: Marcus Books, 1985. (Look at chapter 12 on symbolism, sexuality and love.)

MacLaine, Shirley. *Going Within.* New York: Bantam Books, 1991. (Look at chapter 11 for a discussion on sex and the chakras.)

McGarey, William and Gladys McGarey. *Edgar Cayce's Readings on Home and Marriage.* New York: Bantam Books, 1987. (Look at Chapter 1 on sexual energy and choice and chapter 4 on choosing your partner.)

Puryear, Herbert B. *The Edgar Cayce Primer.* New York: Bantam Books, 1982. (See chapter 21 for a discussion of sex and the spiritual path.)

___. *Sex and The Spiritual Path*. New York: St. Martin's Paperbacks, 1999. Ryerson, Kevin and Stephanie Harolde. *Spirit Communication: The Soul's Path*. New York: Bantam Books, 1991. (See Part 3, chapter 1, pages 115 to 132 for a discussion of soul mates.)

Stern, Jess. *Soulmates*. New York: Bantam Books, 1985.

Todeschi, Kevin J. *Edgar Cayce on Soul Mates*. Virginia Beach: A.R.E. Press, 2001. (Highly recommended book on the dynamics of soul attraction.)

Yogananda, Paramahansa. *Where there is Light*. Los Angeles: Self-Realization Fellowship, 1989. (See chapter 11, pages 137 to 141 on essentials of marriage.)

Zukav, Gary. *The Seat of the Soul*. New York: Fireside Books, 1990. (See Chapter 8, pages 123 to 127 for a discussion on spiritual partnerships.)

The Meaning of Life

Dyer, Wayne W. *Your Sacred Self*. New York: HarperCollins Publishers, 1995. (Good book on qualities required for a happy life.)

Frejer, Ernest B. *The Edgar Cayce Companion*. Virginia Beach: A.R.E. Press, 1997. (Excellent book containing the important readings of Edgar Cayce.)

MacLaine, Shirley. *Out on a Limb*. New York: Bantam Books, 1984. (Highly recommended book on an amazing journey of self-discovery.)

Pendleton, Don and Linda. *To Dance with Angels*. New York: Zebra Books, 1992. (Good book which answers many questions on spiritual and physical life.)

Puryear, Herbert B. *The Edgar Cayce Primer*. New York: Bantam Books, 1982. (See chapter 8, pages 66 to76 for a discussion on "Why we are here?" Also look at chapter 14 on soul development.)

___. *Reflections on the Path*. New York: Bantam Books, 1986. (See pages 60 to 73 for a discussion on our soul's quest for wholeness.)

Roman, Sanaya. *Living with Joy*. Tiburon: H.J Kramer Inc., 1986.

____. *Spiritual Growth: Being Your Higher Self*. Tiburon: H.J Kramer Inc., 1989.

Ryerson, Kevin and Stephanie Harolde. *Spirit Communication: The Soul's Path*. New York: Bantam Books, 1991. (See Part 2, Chapter 3, pages 79 to 85 on a discussion of our life purpose).

Simonson, Valerie. *Orange Socks: How a Yuppie Goes Yogi*. Calgary: Eternal Giving Inc., 1997. (A yuppie's journey for spiritual happiness leads her to Raja Yoga.)

Thurston, Mark. *Soul-Purpose: Discovering and Fulfilling Your Destiny*. San Francisco:Harper & Row, 1989. (See Introduction and chapter 1, pages 3 to 32 for "discovering the meaning of life."

Todeschi, Kevin J. *Soul Development*. Virginia Beach: A.R.E. Press, 2000. (Book answers many meaning of life questions using historical cases and contemporary examples.)

Meditation and prayer

Benson, Herbert with Marg Stark. *Timeless Healing: The Power and Biology of Belief*. New York: Fireside Books, 1997. (See chapter 6 on the positive effects of the "Relaxation Response."

Bethards, Betty. *Techniques for Health and Wholeness*. Novato: Inner Light Foundation, 1985. (See chapter 4 on healing yourself using meditative techniques.)

____. *Be Your Own Guru*. Petaluma: Inner Light Foundation, 1991. (See chapter 5 for a good discussion on meditation and its benefits.)

Chopra, Deepak. *Creating Health*. Boston: Houghton Mifflin Company, 1991. (See Chapter 35 for benefits of Transcendental Meditation. See chapter 37, page 216 for study by Dr. Candace Borland.)

De Angelis, Barbara. *Real Moments*. New York: Dell Publishing, 1995. (See part 4 for everyday meditation and spiritual techniques.)

Denniston, Denise and Peter McWilliams. *The TM Book*. New York: Warner books, 1975. (Excellent book on the benefits of Transcendental Meditation.)

Finch, Raymond. *The Power of Prayer*. Boca Raton: American Media Mini Mags, Inc., 2001. (A 66-page mini-magazine on evidence and methods of prayer.)

Fuller, Elizabeth. *Everyone is Psychic*. New York: Crown Publishers, Inc., 1989. (See Chapter 1 on preparing for meditation. See chapter 2 for some exercises.)

Gawain, Shakti. *Creative Visualization*. New York: Bantam Books, 1982. (Good read. Look at part 3 for meditations and affirmations.)

Goldstein, John and Manuela Soares. *The Joy Within: A Beginner's Guide to Meditation*. New York: Prentice Hall Press, 1990.

Howard, Vernon. *Mystic Path to Cosmic Power*. New York: Parker Publishing Company, Inc., 1967. (See chapter 7 on "How to stop heartache and suffering.")

Krishnamurti, Jiddu. *Meditations*. Boston: Shambhala Publications, Inc., 1979. (Excellent pocket book. See page 2 for description of nature as a meditation.)

LeShan, Lawrence. *How to Meditate*. New York: Bantam Books, 1988. (Good read. Describes physiological and psychological effects of meditations. Also gives some basic types of meditations.)

MacLaine, Shirley. *Going Within*. New York: Bantam Books, 1991. (Look at chapter 4 for an introduction to meditation.)

Mann, John and Lar Short. *The Body of Light*. New York: Globe Press Books, Inc., 1990. (See part 1 which describes the Buddhist, Hindu and other religious traditions perspective of the soul.)

Matthews, Dale with Connie Clark. *The Faith Factor*. New York: Viking Books, 1998. (See chapter 9, pages 199 to 201 on a scientific study of prayer.)

Puryear, Herbert B. *The Edgar Cayce Primer*. New York: Bantam Books, 1982. (See chapter 1 for a discussion on levels of consciousness. See chapters 17 and 18 on benefits of meditation and prayer.)

____. *Reflections on the Path*. New York: Bantam Books, 1986. (See Pages 82 to 96 for a discussion on the healing effects of meditation.)

Puryear, Herbert B. and Mark A. Thurston. *Meditation and the Mind of Man*. Virginia Beach: A.R.E. Press, 1988. (Excellent read. Look at chapter 2 on the nature of the mind and chapter 4 on meditation.)

Yogananda, Paramahansa. *Where there is Light*. Los Angeles: Self-Realization Fellowship, 1989. (See Chapter 7 on how to reduce stress, worry and fear and how to achieve inner peace.)

Yogi, Maharishi Mahesh. *Science of Being and Art of Living: Transcendental Meditation*. New York: Signet Books, 1988. (See especially Section 1, pages 44 to 53 for an excellent explanation of the principles of Transcendental Meditation.)

Other Important Books

The Meaning of the Glorious Koran. Translation by Mohammed Marmaduke Pickthall, New York: Mentor Books, No Date.

The Holy Bible: New International Version, Grand Rapids: Zondervan Publishing House, 1984.

Mentors

Biographies of Mentors

Bushrui, Suheil and Joe Jenkins. *Kahlil Gibran: Man and Poet*. Oxford: Oneworld Publications, 1998. (Great book on a wise poet, artist and mystic.)

Lutyens, Mary. *The Life and Death of Krishnamurti*. London: Rider Publishers, 1991.

Sugrue, Thomas. *There is a River: The Story of Edgar Cayce*. Virginia Beach: A.R.E. Press, 1992. (Excellent autobiography of the great psychic.)

Yogananda, Paramahansa. *Autobiography of a Yogi*. Los Angeles: Self-Realization Fellowship, 1990. (Superb book about the spiritual experiences and path of this great teacher.)

Mentors who teach self-awareness and spiritual concepts

Cayce, Edgar. Any books by Cayce are highly recommended.

Chopra, Deepak. *Return of the Rishi*. Boston: Houghton Mifflin Company, 1988.

___. *Quantum Healing*. New York: Bantam Books, 1990.

___. *Creating Health*. Boston: Houghton Mifflin Company, 1991.

Krishnamurti, Jiddu. *The First and Last Freedom*. San Francisco: HarperCollins Publishers, 1975.

___. *Truth and Actuality*. San Francisco: Harper & Row Publishers, 1980.

___. *The Awakening of Intelligence*. San Francisco: Harper & Row Publishers, 1987.

___. *You Are The World*. New York: Harper & Row Publishers, 1989

MacLaine, Shirley. *Out on a Limb*. New York: Bantam Books, 1984.

___. *It's All in the Playing*. New York: Bantam Books, 1987.

___. *Dancing in the Light*. New York: Bantam Books, 1991.

___. *The Camino*. New York: Pocket Books, 2000.

Moody Jr., Raymond A. *Life After Life*. New York: Bantam Books, 1976.

___. *Reflections on Life After Life*. New York: Bantam Books, 1978.

___. *The Light Beyond*. New York: Bantam Books, 1989.

Morse, Melvin with Paul Perry. *Closer to the Light*. New York: Ivy Books, 1991.

___. *Transformed by the Light*. New York: Ivy Books, 1994.

Robbins, Anthony. *Unlimited Power*. New York: Fawcett Columbine Books, 1986.

___. *Awaken the Giant Within*. New York: Summit Books, 1991.

Ryerson, Kevin and Stephanie Harolde. *Spirit Communication: The Soul's Path*. New York: Bantam Books, 1991.

Yogananda, Paramahansa. *Man's Eternal Quest*. Los Angeles: Self-Realization Fellowship, 1988.

___. *Where there is Light*. Los Angeles: Self-Realization Fellowship, 1989.

___. *The Divine Romance*. Los Angeles: Self-Realization Fellowship, 1992.

Mentors who are spiritual poets

Gibran, Kahlil. *The Prophet*. New York: Alfred A. Knopf, Inc., 2000. (Excellent book on poetry by a great philosopher and artist.)

Rumi, Jelaluddin. Translation by Coleman Barks. *The Essential Rumi*. Edison: Castle Books, 1997. (Great spiritual poetry by the 13th century mystic.)

Mind Over Body

Chopra, Deepak. *Return of the Rishi*. Boston: Houghton Mifflin Company, 1988.

___. *Quantum Healing*. New York: Bantam Books, 1990.

___. *Creating Health*. Boston: Houghton Mifflin Company, 1991.

Benson, Herbert with Marg Stark. *Timeless Healing: The Power and Biology of Belief*. New York: Fireside Books, 1997.

McGarey, William. *In Search of Healing*. New York: Perigee Books, 1996. (See chapter 12 for a discussion on healing, regeneration and longevity. See chapter 15 on faith and illness.)

___. *Healing Miracles: Using Your Body Energies*. San Francisco: Harper & Row, Publishers, 1988.

McGarey, Gladys Taylor with Jess Stearn. *The Physician Within You*. Deerfield Beach: Health Communications Inc., 1997.

Mein, Eric A. *Keys To Health: Holistic Approaches to Healing*. New York: St. Martin's Paperbacks, 1995.

Matthews, Dale with Connie Clark. *The Faith Factor*. New York: Viking Books, 1998.

Myatt, Dana. *A Physician's Diary*. Virginia Beach: A.R.E. Press, 1994. (See chapter 10 on the importance of diet and a healthy mind.)

Oz, Mehmet. *Healing from the Heart*. New York: Plume Books, 1999. (A leading surgeon combines Eastern and Western healing techniques.)

Puryear, Herbert B. *The Edgar Cayce Primer*. New York: Bantam Books, 1982. (See chapter 15 on how attitudes and emotions affect our health. Also see Chapter 20 on holistic healing.)

___. *Reflections on the Path*. New York: Bantam Books, 1986. (See Pages 146 to 163 for a discussion on psychosomatic relationships.)

Sanders Jr., Pete A. *You are Psychic*. New York: Fawcett Columbine Books, 1990. (See Chapter 7 for a good discussion on benefits of self-healing. Pages 185 to 187 have an example of one woman's success over cancer.)

Sinard, John H. "Y2K Revisited: A Human Component?" in *The Journal of the American Medical Association*, April 4, 2001.

Siegel, Bernie S. *Peace, Love & Healing*. New York: Harper & Row Publishers, 1989.

___. *Love, Medicine & Miracles*. New York: HarperPerennial Publishers, 1990.

Near Death and Out of Body Experiences
BBC News Online, Health Section. *Evidence of "Life After Death."* United Kingdom. October 23, 2000.

Berman, Phillip L. *The Journey Home*. New York: Pocket Books, 1996. (Interesting stories of near death experiences.)

Bro, Harmon H. *Edgar Cayce: On Religion and Psychic Experience*. New York: Warner Books, 1988. (See Chapter 8 on out of body experiences.)

Brinkley, Dannion with Paul Perry. *Saved by the Light*. New York: HarperPaperbacks, 1995. (Fascinating account of a near death experience)

___. *At Peace in the Light*. New York: HarperCollins Publishers, 1995.

Eadie, Betty J. *Embraced by the Light*. New York: Bantam Books, 1994. (A good book by a person who had a near death experience.)

___. *The Awakening Heart*. New York: Pocket Books, 1996.

Greenhouse, Herbert B. *The Astral Journey*. New York: Avon Books, 1976. (Interesting book on out of body experiences.)

Lund, David H. *Death And Consciousness*. New York: Ballantine Books, 1989. (See Chapter 8 on out of body experiences.)

MacLaine, Shirley. *Out on a Limb.* New York: Bantam Books, 1984. (Look at chapter 12, pages 168 to 174 on Peter Seller's near death experience.)

Monroe, Robert A. *Journeys Out of The Body.* New York: Dolphin Books, 1977.

___. Far Journeys. New York: Doubleday, 1985.

Moody Jr., Raymond A. *Life After Life.* New York: Bantam Books, 1976.

___. *Reflections on Life After Life.* New York: Bantam Books, 1978.

___. *The Light Beyond.* New York: Bantam Books, 1989. (These three books on near death experiences are highly recommended.)

Morse, Melvin with Paul Perry. *Closer to the Light.* New York: Ivy Books, 1991. (Pediatrician looks at near death experiences of children.)

___. *Transformed by the Light.* New York: Ivy Books, 1994.

Rogo, D.Scott. *Leaving the Body.* New York: Prentice Hall Press, 1986.

Ryerson, Kevin and Stephanie Harolde. *Spirit Communication: The Soul's Path.* New York: Bantam Books, 1991. (See part 2, Chapter 2, pages 71 to72 for an out of body experiment.)

Steiger, Brad. *One with the Light.* New York: Signet Books, 1994. (Authentic cases of near death experiences.)

Reincarnation

Anderson, George and Andrew Barone. *Lessons from the Light.* New York: G.P. Putnam's Sons, 1999. (See Chapter 4 for an interesting discussion on terminal illness and reincarnation.)

Cerminara, Gina. *Many Mansions.* New York: Signet Books, 1967.

___. *Many Lives, Many Loves.* New York: Signet Books, 1974.

___. *The World Within.* Virginia Beach: A.R.E. Press, 1988. (Good books on karma and reincarnation.)

Chadwick, Gloria. *Discovering Your Past Lives.* Chicago: Contemporary Books, 1988. (Look at chapter 9 for a discussion on our present life as an indicator of the past.)

Fisher, Joe. *The Case for Reincarnation*. Toronto: Collins Publishers, 1984. (Highly recommended. Especially look at Chapter 2 about children who claimed to be reincarnated. See chapter 7 on reincarnation and Christianity.)

Fuller, Elizabeth. *Everyone is Psychic*. New York: Crown Publishers, Inc., 1989. (See Chapter 5 for an interesting discussion on reincarnation and past lives.) Karpinski, Gloria D. *Where Two Worlds Touch: Spiritual Rites of Passage*. New York: Ballantine Books, 1990. (Look at pages 88 to 123 for a good introduction to reincarnation.)

Langley, Noel. *Edgar Cayce on Reincarnation*. New York: Warner Books, 1988.

Lenz, Frederick. *Lifetimes: True Accounts of Reincarnation*. New York:

Fawcett Crest Books, 1991.

Moody Jr., Raymond A with Paul Perry. *Coming Back*. New York: Bantam Books, 1992. (Dr. Moody examines past life regression.)

Montgomery, Ruth. *Here and Hereafter*. New York: Fawcett Crest Books, 1991. (See chapter 6 for an interesting discussion on what occurs between lives.)

Puryear, Herbert B. *The Edgar Cayce Primer*. New York: Bantam Books, 1982. (See chapter 3 for a very good discussion on reincarnation.)

___. *Reflections on the Path*. New York: Bantam Books, 1986. (See Pages 46 to 59 for a discussion on reincarnation, psychology and Christianity.)

Ryerson, Kevin and Stephanie Harolde. *Spirit Communication: The Soul's Path*. New York: Bantam Books, 1991. (See Part 3, Chapter 3, pages 247 to 250 on past lives.)

Sharma, I.C. *Cayce, Karma & Reincarnation*. Wheaton: Quest books, 1975. (See Chapter 6, pages 74 to 89 on nature and purpose of reincarnation.)

Shelley, Violet M. *Reincarnation Unnecessary*. Virginia Beach: A.R.E. Press, 1979. (See Chapter 4 for a discussion on important spiritual attributes.)

Sparrow, Lynn Elwell. *Reincarnation: Claiming Your Past, Creating Your Future*. New York: St. Martin's Paperbacks, 1995. (Excellent book on reincarnation.)

Steiger, Brad. *You Will Live Again*. New York: Dell Publishing, 1978. (Good case histories on reincarnation.)

Sutphen, Dick. *Finding Your Answers Within*. New York: Pocket Books, 1989. (See chapter 4 for examples of past life regressions.)

Todeschi, Kevin J. *Edgar Cayce on the Akashic Records*. Virginia Beach: A.R.E. Press, 1998. (See Chapter 3 on recognizing insights from the past.)

___. *Soul Development*. Virginia Beach: A.R.E. Press, 2000. (See Chapter 3, for examples on how reincarnation affects current lives.)

Responsibility for the future

Bethards, Betty. *Be Your Own Guru*. Petaluma: Inner Light Foundation, 1991. (See chapter 6 for a discussion on our problems in the past and our responsibilities and potential for the future.)

Black, J. Anderson. *Nostradamus: The Prophecies*. London: Greenwich Editions, 1998.

Childs, Christopher. *The Spirit's Terrain*. Boston: Beacon Press Books, 1998. (A social and spiritual book by an environmentalist.)

Doig, Desmond. *Mother Teresa: Her People and her Work*. Glasgow: Fount Paperbacks, 1988. (Mother Teresa's words of wisdom and dedication to the poor of Calcutta).

Mann, A.T. *Millennium Prophecies*. Rockport: Element Books Inc., 1995.

Robbins, Anthony. *Awaken the Giant Within*. New York: Summit Books, 1991. (See part 4 for a discussion of our worldly responsibilities.)

Thurston, Mark. *Edgar Cayce Predicts*. Virginia Beach: A.R.E. Press, 1991.

Todeschi, Kevin J. *Soul Development*. Virginia Beach: A.R.E. Press, 2000. (See chapter 8 on how we can make the world a better place.)

Spirit Guides and Angels

Belhayes, Iris. *Spirit Guides*. San Diego: ACS Publications, 1993. (Good book on spirit guides.)

Fuller, Elizabeth. *Everyone is Psychic*. New York: Crown Publishers, Inc., 1989. (See chapter 7 on spirit guides and creative assistance.)

Puryear, Herbert B. *Reflections on the Path*. New York: Bantam Books, 1986. (See pages 97 to 115 for a discussion on guides and gurus.)

Ridall, Kathryn. *Channeling: How To Reach Out To Your Spirit Guides*. New York: Bantam Books, 1988. (See chapter 3 for a discussion on spirit guides.)

Ronner, John. *Do You Have a Guardian Angel?* Murfreesboro: Mamre Press, 1992. (Highly recommended book on angels.)

Ryerson, Kevin and Stephanie Harolde. *Spirit Communication: The Soul's Path*. New York: Bantam Books, 1991. (See part 3, Chapter 1, pages 132 to 143 on spirit guides and teachers.)

Steiger, Brad. *Guardian Angels and Spirit Guides*. New York: Plume Books, 1995. (True and interesting accounts with beings from the other side.)

Sutphen, Dick. *Finding Your Answers Within*. New York: Pocket Books, 1989. (See chapter 3 for examples on communication with spirit guides.)

Other Books

The Meaning of the Glorious Koran. Translation by Mohammed Marmaduke Pickthall, New York: Mentor Books, No Date.

The Holy Bible: New International Version. Grand Rapids: Zondervan Publishing House, 1984.

Suicide

Anderson, George and Andrew Barone. *Lessons from the Light*. New York: G.P. Putnam's Sons, 1999. (See Chapter 6 for an interesting discussion about the negative implications of suicide from souls who passed on — highly recommended)

Fairchilde, Lily. *Song of the Phoenix*. New York: St. Martin's Press, 1997. (See chapter 8 about a soul who committed suicide — highly recommended)

Cerminara, Gina. *Many Mansions*. New York: Signet Books, 1967. (Look at Chapter 14, pages 131 to 135 for karmic results of suicide.)

Moody Jr., Raymond A. *Reflections on Life After Life*. New York: Bantam Books, 1978. (See chapter 3 for an interesting discussion on suicide from people who had near death experiences.)

Richelieu, Peter. *A Soul's Journey*. London: The Aquarian Press, 1989. (See Chapter 9, pages 142 to 143 for a discussion of the negative ramifications of suicide.)

Van Praagh, James. *Talking To Heaven: A Medium's Message of Life After Death*. New York: Dutton Books, 1997. (See chapter 7 for an interesting discussion on suicide from souls that have passed on.)

UFOS

Anka, Darryl and Luana Ewing. *Bashar: Blueprint for Change*. Seattle: New Solutions Publishing, 1991. (See part 3 for an interesting discussion on extraterrestrials.)

Fiore, Edith. *Encounters*. New York: Ballantine Books, 1990. (Case studies of fourteen abductions.)

Hopkins, Budd. *Intruders*. New York: Ballantine Books, 1992. (Interesting case of abduction.)

Jung, C.G., Translation by R.F.C. Hull. *Flying Saucers: A Modern Myth of Things Seen in the Skies*. New York: MJF Books, 1978. (Jung's perspectives on UFOs.)

MacLaine, Shirley. *Out on a Limb*. New York: Bantam Books, 1984. (See Chapters 15, 17, 18, 19, 22 and 23 for interesting references to UFOs.)

___. *The Camino*. New York: Pocket Books, 2000. (See Chapter 15 for an interesting discussion on the impact of extraterrestrials on our past history.)

Strieber, Whitley. *Confirmation*. New York: St. Martin's Press, 1998. (Interesting book on the UFO phenomenon, close encounters and abductions.)

Pendleton, Don and Linda. *To Dance with Angels*. New York: Zebra Books, 1992. (Look at Chapter 9 for an interesting discussion on our spiritual connection to extraterrestrials.)

About the Author

Riaz Manji was born in Tanzania, East Africa. In 1971, when he was thirteen years old, he moved to England and four years later, to his present home in Canada. In 1981, he completed a degree in Commerce and then successfully worked in the oil and gas industry for more than eighteen years. Manji started writing *A Handbook for the Spiritual Traveler* while taking care of his mother, who was dying of cancer. This experience, as well as other significant events in his life, caused him to search deeply for an understanding of the human spirit. Manji has spent over a decade probing into universal concerns such as the meaning of our life here on Earth and the immortal nature of the soul. In *A Handbook for the Spiritual Traveler*, Manji presents a summary of his findings in an easy-to-read and engaging manner. He hopes that his *Handbook* will assist other spiritual travelers in their journeys. Riaz Manji lives in Calgary, Alberta, Canada.

Order Form

A Handbook for the Spiritual Traveler is available in most major bookstores (ISBN 0-9730535-0-X). Check www.steppingstonepublishing.com for bookstores and online retailers.

A Handbook for the Spiritual Traveler can also be ordered by completing the following order form. Please send a cheque or money order to:

Stepping Stone Publishing
P.O. Box 84122
Market Mall RPO
Calgary, Alberta, Canada
T3A 5C4

CANADA		US AND OVERSEAS (in US Funds)	
_____ copies @ $18.95	$_____	_____ copies @ $12.95	$_____
Shipping & Handling (1st book) $4.00	$_____	Shipping & Handling (1st book) US - $4.00 Overseas - $6.00	$_____
Add $2.00 for each additional book	$_____	Additional books US, add $2.50/book. Overseas, add $5.00/bk.	$_____
Subtotal	$_____		$_____
GST (7%)	$_____		
Total Enclosed ($CDN)	$_____	Total Enclosed ($US)	$_____

Shipping & Handling rates are effective for the year 2002. Please visit www.steppingstonepublishing.com for possible changes. **Please include your name, complete address, email address and phone number**. Allow 4-6 weeks for delivery.

For any questions, comments or feedback, contact the publisher at the above mailing address, or at www.steppingstonepublishing.com or email: info@steppingstonepublishing.com

Riaz looks forward to your comments. To contact him, write to the above mailing address, visit www.steppingstonepublishing.com or www.riazmanji.com or email riaz@steppingstonepublishing.com.